Lecture Notes in Computer Science   11009

Commenced Publication in 1973
Founding and Former Series Editors:
Gerhard Goos, Juris Hartmanis, and Jan van Leeuwen

More information about this series at http://www.springer.com/series/7412

Alicia Fornés · Bart Lamiroy (Eds.)

Graphics Recognition

Current Trends and Evolutions

12th IAPR International Workshop, GREC 2017
Kyoto, Japan, November 9–10, 2017
Revised Selected Papers

 Springer

Editors
Alicia Fornés ⓘ
Computer Vision Center
Autonomous University of Barcelona
Bellaterra, Barcelona, Spain

Bart Lamiroy ⓘ
Université de Lorraine
Nancy, France

ISSN 0302-9743   ISSN 1611-3349 (electronic)
Lecture Notes in Computer Science
ISBN 978-3-030-02283-9   ISBN 978-3-030-02284-6 (eBook)
https://doi.org/10.1007/978-3-030-02284-6

Library of Congress Control Number: 2018958464

LNCS Sublibrary: SL6 – Image Processing, Computer Vision, Pattern Recognition, and Graphics

This Springer imprint is published by the registered company Springer Nature Switzerland AG
The registered company address is: Gewerbestrasse 11, 6330 Cham, Switzerland

Preface

As in previous editions, the 12th IAPR International Workshop on Graphics Recognition (GREC 2017) was organized by the IAPR TC-10 (Technical Committee on Graphics Recognition). It took place in November in Kyoto (Japan), just before the 14th International Conference on Document Analysis and Recognition (ICDAR 2017).

As usual, the GREC workshop provided an excellent opportunity for researchers and practitioners at all levels of experience to meet colleagues and to share new ideas and knowledge about graphics recognition methods, applied, among others, to engineering drawings, maps, architectural plans, comics, musical scores, mathematical notation, tables, diagrams, etc. Instead of being a mini-conference, GREC aims for its unique and creative workshop atmosphere, through highly dynamic interactive and productive sessions. The workshop enjoyed strong participation from researchers in both industry and academia.

As in previous editions, the program was organized in a single-track two-day workshop. It comprised several sessions dedicated to specific topics related to graphics in document analysis and graphic recognition. Each session began with an introductory talk by the session chairs, who introduced the topic, stated the current open challenges, put the presented talks in a more global perspective, and in many cases, highlighted links and relations between the papers of each session. This introduction was then followed by short scientific presentations of results or solutions to some of these questions. Each session was concluded by a panel discussion, which became a highly interactive debate between the audience and the presenters of the papers.

In this edition, 27 papers were presented, followed by highly interactive discussions. On the first day, GREC hosted a record-breaking 110 participants. Unlike with other editions, we also included in the program the IAPR invited talk and the discussion groups.

The IAPR invited speaker was Prof. Ichiro Fujinaga, Chair of the Music Technology Area at the Schulich School of Music at McGill University. He has been the acting director of the Center for Interdisciplinary Research in Music Media and Technology (CIRMMT) and a faculty member at the Peabody Conservatory of Music at the Johns Hopkins University. In his talk "A Retrospective on Optical Music Recognition Research," he reviewed the progress of optical music recognition (OMR) research from its inception in the late 1960s to the present. His talk included an overview of the history of Gamera and other non-commercial software developments, including the software developed within his research projects at McGill University.

On the first day, Bart Lamiroy also presented the Engineering Drawing Challenge II, the continuation of the challenge presented at GREC 2015 in Nancy. It included the presentation of the collection of 800 engineering drawings, available on the Lehigh University DAE server.

At the end of the first day, we enjoyed discussion groups, where the level of interaction was very intense and rich. It consisted of small-group discussions on topics of special interest to attendees. We split up into several groups to discuss graphics recognition topics, such as structures and relations in the deep learning age, optical music recognition, how to get over the bottleneck of annotated data for learning approaches, and the engineering drawing challenge. On the second day, a spokesperson of each group summarized the results of their discussions to all GREC attendees. Some of these groups also had volunteers who wrote a short summary report that is included in this volume.

At the end of the second day, we had the final panel discussion, led by Josep Lladós, a senior member of our community and one of the former TC10 chairs, who presented a retrospective of the last 20 years of GREC workshops and his vision concerning the future of the community.

The current proceedings contain ten reviewed and extended selected papers, the Engineering Drawing Challenge II, several reports summarizing the discussion groups, and the final panel discussion.

The GREC organizers would like to thank all participants for the highly interactive GREC workshop, with many fruitful discussions on graphics recognition topics.

August 2018   Alicia Fornés
                                                                                                              Bart Lamiroy

Organization

General Chairs

Alicia Fornés	Computer Vision Center, Spain
Bart Lamiroy	Université de Lorraine, France

Program Chairs

Alicia Fornés	Computer Vision Center, Spain
Bart Lamiroy	Université de Lorraine, France

TC-10 Steering Committee

Syed Saqib Bukhari	German Research Center for Artificial Intelligence (DFKI), Germany
Jean-Christophe Burie	University of La Rochelle, France
Alicia Fornés	Computer Vision Center, Spain
Motoi Iwata	Osaka Prefecture University, Sakai, Japan
Bart Lamiroy	Université de Lorraine, France
Rafael Dueire Lins	Federal University of Pernambuco, Brazil
Josep Lladós	Computer Vision Center, Spain
Jean-Marc Ogier	University of La Rochelle, France
K. C. Santosh	University of South Dakota, USA

Program Committee

Eric Anquetil	INSA/IRISA, France
Partha Bhowmick	Indian Institute of Technology Kharagpur, India
Jean-Christophe Burie	University of La Rochelle, France
Jorge Calvo-Zaragoza	Universidad de Alicante, Spain
Bhabatosh Chanda	Indian Statistical Institute, India
Mickael Coustaty	University of La Rochelle, France
Gunther Drevin	North-West University, South Africa
Ichiro Fujinaga	McGill University, Canada
Petra Gomez-Krämer	University of La Rochelle, France
Pierre Héroux	Université de Rouen Normanie, France
Christoph Langenhan	Technische Universität München, Germany
Josep Lladós	Computer Vision Center, Spain
Muhammad Muzzamil Luqman	University of La Rochelle, France
Sekhar Mandal	IIEST, Shibpur, India
Jean-Marc Ogier	University of La Rochelle, France

Umapada Pal	Indian Statistical Institute, Kolkata, India
Oriol Ramos Terrades	Universitat Autònoma de Barcelona - Computer Vision Center, Spain
Christophe Rigaud	University of La Rochelle, France
K. C. Santosh	University of South Dakota, USA
Richard Zanibbi	Rochester Institute of Technology, USA

Session Chairs

Syed Saqib Bukhari	German Research Center for Artificial Intelligence (DFKI), Germany
Jorge Calvo-Zaragoza	Universitat Politècnica de Valencia, Spain
Mickael Coustaty	University of La Rochelle, France
Francisco Cruz	University of La Rochelle, France
Gunther Drevin	North-West University, South Africa
Véronique Eglin	Université de Lyon, France
Nina Hirata	University of São Paulo, Brazil
Josep Lladós	Computer Vision Center, Spain
Muhammad Muzzamil Luqman	University of La Rochelle, France
Wataru Ohyama	Kyushu University, Japan
Christophe Rigaud	University of La Rochelle, France
Richard Zanibbi	Rochester Institute of Technology, USA

Contents

Analysis and Detection of Diagrams

Automated Extraction of Data from Binary Phase Diagrams for Discovery of Metallic Glasses

Bhargava Urala Kota[1]([✉]), Rathin Radhakrishnan Nair[1], Srirangaraj Setlur[1],
Aparajita Dasgupta[2], Scott Broderick[2], Venu Govindaraju[1],
and Krishna Rajan[2]

[1] Department of Computer Science and Engineering, University at Buffalo,
State University of New York, Buffalo, NY, USA
{buralako,rathinra,setlur,govind}@buffalo.edu
[2] Department of Materials Design and Innovation, University at Buffalo,
State University of New York, Buffalo, NY, USA
{adasgupt,scottbro,krajan3}@buffalo.edu

Abstract. We present a study on automated analysis of phase diagrams that attempts to lay the groundwork for a large-scale, indexable, digitized database of phases at different thermodynamic conditions and compositions for a wide variety of materials. For this work, we concentrate on approximately 80 thermodynamic phase diagrams of binary metallic alloy systems which give phase information of multi-component systems at varied temperatures and mixture ratios. We use image processing techniques to isolate phase boundaries and subsequently extract areas of the same phase. Simultaneously, document analysis techniques are employed to recognize and group the text used to label the phases; text present along the axes is identified so as to map image coordinates (x, y) to physical coordinates. Labels of unlabeled phases are inferred using standard rules. Once a phase diagram is thus digitized we are able to providethe phase of all materials present in our database at any given temperature and alloy mixture ratio. Using the digitized data, more complex queries may also be supported in the future. We evaluate our system by measuring the correctness of labeling of phase regions and obtain an accuracy of about 94%. Our work was then used to detect eutectic points and angles on the contour graphs which are important for some material design strategies, which aided in identifying 38 previously unexplored metallic glass forming compounds - an active topic of research in materials sciences.

1 Introduction

Traditionally, document based information retrieval systems have focused on using data from text and, to a lesser extent, from images. They do not extract, analyze or index the content in document graphics (non-pictorial images in articles). Scientific documents often present important information via graphics and

© Springer Nature Switzerland AG 2018
A. Fornés and B. Lamiroy (Eds.): GREC 2017, LNCS 11009, pp. 3–16, 2018.
https://doi.org/10.1007/978-3-030-02284-6_1

little work has been done in the document analysis community to address this gap. The graphics present in documents are predominantly in the form of line, scatter plots, bar charts, etc. [1]. Most current techniques for interacting with graphics in documents involve user provided metadata. Information graphics are a valuable knowledge resource that should be retrievable from a digital library and graphics should be taken into account when summarizing a multimodal document for indexing and retrieval [2]. Automated analysis of graphics in documents can facilitate comprehensive document image analysis, and the information gathered can support the evidence obtained from the text data and allow for inferences and analysis that would not have otherwise been possible [3]. In this work, the primary focus is on analyzing and interpreting information contained in phase diagrams which are critical for design within the Materials Science and Engineering community.

Phase diagrams serve as a mapping of phase stability in the context of extrinsic variables such as chemical composition with respect to temperature and/or pressure and therefore provide the equilibrium phase compositions and ratios under variable thermodynamic conditions. The geometrical characteristics of phase diagrams, including the shape of phase boundaries and positions of phase boundary junctions have fundamental thermodynamic origins. Hence they serve as a visual signature of the nature of thermo-chemical properties of alloys. The design of alloys for instance, relies on inspection of many such documented phase diagrams and this is usually a manual process. Our objective is to develop an automated document recognition tool that can process large quantities of phase diagrams in order to support user queries which, in turn, facilitate the simultaneous screening of a large number of materials without loss of information.

Further, from the phase diagram images, we readily identify specific types of phase boundary junctions, known as 'eutectic points'. We have used this test case to show that we can characterize the shape of eutectic points, and provide a meaning to the term 'deep eutectic'. Deep eutectics are known to be critical for the formation of metallic glasses (i.e. metallic systems without crystalline order), although previously no clear meaning of deep eutectic had been defined in terms of identifying new compounds [4].

Phase diagrams need specific attention primarily because of the way the information is embedded into the diagram. The lines in a phase diagram are not of a continuously changing value like in a line plot, but instead represent a boundary. A phase diagram cannot be expressed by a simple table like most line plots, bar charts etc. Further, text can appear in different orientations and subsequently associating the text with the phase regions (and sometimes vertical lines) is an added complexity that is non-trivial and essential to the final interpretation by materials science domain experts. These characteristics underline the necessity for having a targeted approach to handling this particular class of diagrams.

For our study, we randomly select a small subset of phase diagrams of binary metallic alloy systems where the X-axis is molar fraction percentage and the Y axis is temperature. The goal of our study is to create a database, where given a temperature value and molar fraction percentage for a particular alloy, the

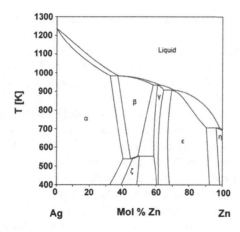

Fig. 1. A typical phase diagram with labeled boundaries.

database returns the phases of the alloy. A typical phase diagram is shown in Fig. 1. Since there are potentially infinite real-valued query points, we evaluate our system on how correctly an entire phase region, i.e., the set of all possible points with the same phase, is labeled.

The rest of the paper is organized as follows: Sect. 2 provides an overview of the related work done for understanding information graphics. Section 3 describes phase diagrams and Sects. 4 through 6 discuss the proposed approach, followed by details of the evaluation metrics and a discussion in Sect. 7.

2   Background

Although graphics analysis and understanding of a variety of diagrams has been addressed in the literature, to the best of our knowledge, no prior work has tackled the problem of analyzing and understanding classes of diagrams with complex semantic interpretation such as phase diagrams. The purpose of graphics in most cases is to display data, including the ones in popular media and research documents. Specifically, in research documents, they serve the purpose of pictorially comparing performance of multiple approaches, and offering objective evaluations of the method proposed in the manuscript. In this section, we discuss some prior work in graphics analysis and understanding. We are primarily interested in analyzing the structure of the graphic and analyzing it to interpret the information present in it. A survey of some of the earliest work in the field of diagram recognition is mentioned in [5], where they discuss the challenges of handling different types of diagrams, the complexity in representing the syntax and semantics, and handling noise. Noise in the graphic makes data extraction difficult, as the data points can be close and hence can be skewed or intersecting. Shahab et al. [6] presented the different techniques that were used to solve the problem of detecting and recognizing text from complex images. Relevant information include understanding the axis labels, legend and the values the plots represent.

Attempts at graphics understanding from scientific plots can be seen in [1, 7] targeting bar charts, and simple line plots [3, 8, 9]. An understanding of the information required to be extracted is a key component in disambiguating the relevant section of a graphic, and [8] tackles the extraction of relevant information from line plots which are one of the more commonly used information graphics in a research setting. Additionally, in [3] the authors propose a method using hough transform and heuristics to identify the axis lines. The rules include the relative position between axis lines, the location of axis lines in a 2-D plot, and the relative length of axis lines in a 2-D plot. The textual information that is embedded into the graphics, such as axes labels and legends, in line plots and bar charts, is also crucial to understanding the graphics. Connected components and boundary/perimeter features [10] have been used to characterize document blocks. [11] discusses methods to extract numerical information in charts. They use a 3 step algorithm to detect text in an image using connected components, detect text lines using hough transform [12], and inter-character distance and character size to identify final text strings followed by Tesseract OCR [13] for text recognition. Color (HSV) based features have also been used to separate plot lines and text/axes [14] for interpretation of line plots that use color to discriminate lines. This study reports results on about 100 plots classified as 'easy' by the authors. They also use a color-based text pixel extraction scheme where the text is present only outside the axes and in the legend.

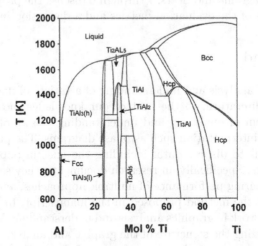

Fig. 2. Example of a challenging phase diagram.

Once the relevant data has been extracted, the next logical step is in connecting them in a coherent manner to interpret the information contained in the chart. [15] discusses the importance of communicative signals, which are information that can be used to interpret bar charts. Some of the signals of interest that represent the information from the graphic include annotations, effort, words in caption, and highlighted components. Allen et. al [16], in one of the earliest works in the area developed a system for deducing the intended meaning of an indirect speech act. In [9], a similar idea is used in understanding line plots by breaking down each line plot into trends and representing each trend by a message. These constituent trend level messages are combined to obtain a holistic message for the line plot.

While phase diagrams belong broadly to the class of plots, they require special treatment due to the complex embedding of information into these diagrams, as explained in the next section. The contour nature of the plot, complex text placement with semantic import, and challenging locations and orientations coupled with the optional presence of other graphic symbols such as arrows that are vital for semantic interpretation of the figure, justify a dedicated exploration of such complex diagrams.

3   Phase Diagrams

Phase diagrams are graphs that are used to show the physical conditions (temperature, pressure, composition) at which thermodynamically distinct phases occur and coexist in materials of interest [17]. A common component in phase diagrams is lines which denote the physical conditions in which two or more phases coexist in equilibrium - these are known as *phase boundaries*. The X and Y axes of a phase diagram typically denote a physical quantity such as temperature, pressure and, in the case of alloys or mixtures, the ratio of components by weight or by molar fraction. As stated earlier, we focus on phase diagrams of binary metal alloys where the X-axis is molar fraction percentage and the Y axis is temperature. In Fig. 1, the blue lines within the plot denote the phase boundaries. All points bounded by a phase boundary represent physical conditions at which the material of interest, in this case an alloy of silver and zinc, occurs in the same phase. The name or label of this phase, for example α in Fig. 1, is typically present somewhere within the phase boundary. The various Greek letters present in the phase diagram represent different types of solid phases (i.e. crystal structures). Positioning within a phase defines the ratio of the different phases, as well as the composition of the phases. All of these characteristics heavily impact the material properties.

We can observe that there are several regions that are unlabeled. These regions represent multi-phase regions and the phases that constitute this mixture are obtained by using the phase labels of the regions to the left and right of the unlabeled region. Additionally, as shown in Fig. 2, in several phase diagrams, labels are sometimes provided to the phase boundary instead of the region. These cases represent intermetallic compositions (ie. the labeled phase exists only at that one composition, thus explaining the vertical line which is labeled). In such cases, the same rule to infer phase labels holds true except we would be using a vertical line on the left or on the right to obtain one of the two phase labels.

4 Overview of Our Approach

From a document analysis perspective, a phase diagram can be seen to consist mainly of alphanumeric text, often with accompanying Greek characters, in vertical and horizontal orientations; bounded regions of uniform phase within the plot; and descriptions of axes and numerical quantities along the axes. As can be seen in Fig. 2, narrow and small phase regions, presence of arrows, text located very close to phase boundaries and different orientations pose steep challenges to the automated analysis. The key steps in automated phase diagram analysis are listed below and will be elaborated in the sections that follow:

- detection and recognition of text used to label phases
- extraction of regions of uniform phases
- association of each phase region to appropriate labels
- detection and recognition of axes text in order to convert image coordinates to physical coordinates and detect elements of the binary alloy

5 Identifying Text and Phase Regions

The phase diagram images that we have considered in this study were obtained from a single source - the Computational Phase Diagram Database [18] from the National Institute of Materials Science, so that the phase labeling, and plot and image styling are consistent. We gathered about 80 different phase diagrams of binary alloys consisting of a number of common transition metals and main group metals. Each image was preprocessed by Otsu thresholding [19] and inverting it, so that background pixels are off and foreground pixels are on. We then extracted contours using the border following algorithm proposed by Suzuki and Abe [20]. The largest contour extracted corresponds to the box that defines the axes and the plot. The contours are then divided into plot (inside the largest contour), and non-plot (outside the largest contour). Plot and non-plot contours were manually annotated using an in-house annotation tool and a database of about 720 phase region contours and about 7100 text region contours were created. This database was divided into a training and validation set in the ratio 4 : 1. We then extracted the following features from the contours:

- Unit normalized coordinates of the contour bounding box
- Bounding box area normalized with respect to image area
- Contour area normalized with respect to area of image
- Convex hull area normalized with respect to area of image
- Ratio of contour area to convex hull area
- Ratio of contour area to bounding box area
- Ratio of convex area to bounding box area
- Contour perimeter normalized with respect to image perimeter
- Orientation, Eccentricity of contour
- Hu invariant moments

The features are designed so as to normalize the effect of large size disparity between phase regions and text regions. Orientation and eccentricity are computed using first and second order image moments of the contour. Hu invariant moments [21] are seven image moments that are invariant to rotation, translation, scale and skew. They are commonly used in object recognition and segmentation [22,23].

Table 1. Confusion matrix for contour classification

%	Phase	Text
Phase	97.60	2.40
Text	0.15	99.85

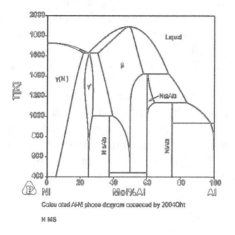

Fig. 3. Classification of text (red) and phase (blue) contours. Best viewed in color. (Color figure online)

The feature vector extracted from the contour has a dimensionality of 20. Features are extracted from training contours and a gradient boosted tree-based classifier is trained to classify between phase contours and text contours. We choose this classifier as we found it to be the most robust to our unbalanced data among other classifiers such as support vector machine (SVM), random forests and neural networks. The number of estimators was chosen to be 1000 and the maximum depth of each tree was fixed at 10 after a grid search. The performance of the trained classifier is evaluated on the validation set. Table 1 shows the confusion matrix obtained after evaluation. We can see that our model is quite proficient at classifying phase and text contours. Figure 3 shows the classification of text and phase contours in one of our phase diagram images. The text contours are marked in red and phase contours are marked blue.

6   Mapping Regions to Labels

After classification of all contours into non-phase and phase, we concentrate on grouping the text contours into words and recognizing the text, so that these word labels can then be mapped to the appropriate phase contours.

6.1   Segmenting Text into Words

As a first step, all text contours that are fully contained within another text contour are eliminated. Then, we sort all of the plot text contours in increasing order of y-coordinate of the centroid cy. A text contour i, whose centroid y-coordinate cy_i value is within a certain threshold H_t^1 from the previous contour $i - 1$ is grouped together as belonging to the same line. Otherwise, it becomes the start of a new line. Once the text contours are grouped into lines, we sort text contours in a single line by the increasing order of x-coordinates of their centroid cx. A text contour i is grouped together as belonging to the same word as the previous contour $i - 1$ if their centroid x-coordinates differ by a value of H_t^2, otherwise it becomes the start of a new word. We fixed the values of H_t^1 as h_{mean}, the average height of all text contour bounding boxes within the plot and H_t^2 as 1.5 × w_{mean}, the average width of text contour bounding boxes in that particular line.

Using this method of line and word grouping works well for horizontally oriented text, however vertically aligned text are still left as isolated contours. In order to group vertical text, we repeat the procedure described above, except we group the text contours by x-coordinate of centroids to obtain vertical text lines and switch to grouping by y-coordinate of centroids to obtain vertical words in each line. We use a different set of thresholds, V_t^1 and V_t^2 respectively. We chose

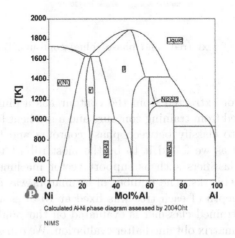

Fig. 4. Grouping of text into vertical (red) and horizontal (blue) words. Best viewed in color. (Color figure online)

the values of V_t^1 as w_{mean}, the average width of all isolated text contour bounding boxes and V_t^2 as $1.5 \times h_{mean}$, the average height of text contour bounding boxes in that particular vertical line.

Some single character text or contours that contain many characters may be left isolated and not grouped into horizontal or vertical lines. These contours are marked as ambiguous. The ambiguity is resolved by rotating the contours 90° in both clockwise and anti-clockwise directions and attempting to recognize the text in all three configurations. The configuration that yields the highest confidence is selected as the right orientation for these contours. Once the correct orientation of all contours is known, we perform OCR on all the words by using the orientation information. For vertically aligned text, we flip the word about the Y-axis, and compare recognition confidence in both directions to finalize the orientation. Figure 4 shows the grouping and orientation of plot text contours of the phase diagram in Fig. 3. Recognition is performed using the Tesseract library [13].

6.2 Detection of Arrows

Since the phase label for phase regions that are small in area cannot be placed within the region, they are usually displayed elsewhere and an arrow is used to indicate the region or line for the phase association. It is therefore necessary to identify arrows in order to accurately match these text contours to the corresponding phase contour. Arrows occur frequently in our dataset and are vital for correct interpretation of the phase diagram as can be seen in Fig. 2. We use a Hough line detector to detect arrows. Since the length of arrows varies in our dataset, we tune the Hough line detector to detect short line segments. Collinear and overlapping line segments are merged to yield the list of arrows in the image. The arrow direction is determined by comparing the center of mass of the arrow and its geometric midpoint. Due to more pixels located at the head of the arrow, we expect the center of mass to be between the head and the midpoint. For every arrow, we find the word region closest to the tail and the phase contour or vertical line closest to the head and these are stored as matched pairs. Figure 5 shows an example of successful arrow detection and corresponding text box association.

6.3 Completing the Mapping

Once the text within the plot is grouped and recognized and the arrows in the image have been dealt with, we proceed to associate the rest of the text labels to the appropriate phase regions and boundary lines. Vertical words are mapped to the nearest unlabeled vertical line by measuring the perpendicular distance between the centroid of the word bounding box and the line. After this, we match phase regions to horizontal text labels by finding the text bounding boxes that are fully contained within the phase region. We resolve conflicts, if any, by giving priority to text labels whose centroid is closest to that of the phase region. Labels for unlabeled phase contours are inferred using the rules described in Sect. 3.

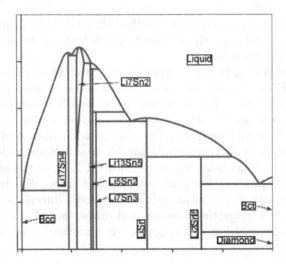

Fig. 5. Arrow detection and corresponding text box association. Best viewed in color. (Color figure online)

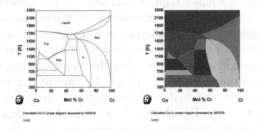

Fig. 6. Extraction of phase contours. Best viewed in color. (Color figure online)

6.4 Handling Text in the Axes

Text grouping, recognition and orientation determination is performed for text contours outside the plot boundary using the same procedure described in Sect. 6. The text regions to the left of the plot box closest to the top-left and bottom left corners are identified and recognized. Using the vertical distance between these two regions as well as the recognized numerals we can easily compute the value of the temperature that corresponds to the top-left and bottom-left corners of the plot box. Thus, we are able to translate the image coordinates (x, y) to the physical coordinates $(molefraction, temperature)$. With this, we will be able to query any required physical coordinate for any binary alloy, convert it to image coordinates and find the phase contour which contains this point and return the label assigned to the contour.

7   Evaluation and Discussion

Despite designing a system which digitizes a phase diagram and returns the phase information of any queried point, we choose to eschew the traditional information retrieval oriented evaluation scheme. Instead, we present our accuracy of phase contour labeling for both cases - labels present within the phase diagram and labels that have to be inferred. This is because, in our case, we could potentially generate an infinite number of real-valued queries within the bounds of the plot axes and each one would have a corresponding phase label response. Depending on the kind of points queried we could have precision and recall numbers skewed to very high or very low accuracy and there would be no guarantee of a fair evaluation of our system. By measuring the accuracy of phase contour labeling, we can therefore obtain a comprehensive idea of the efficacy of our system.

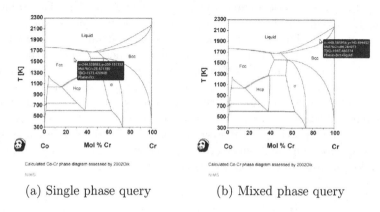

      (a) Single phase query   (b) Mixed phase query

Fig. 7. Demo of our live phase query retrieval system. Best viewed in color. (Color figure online)

To this end, we have annotated the phase diagrams using the LabelMe annotation tool [24]. Expert annotators provided the text labels for all phase contours as well as relevant phase boundaries which were used as ground truth and the accuracy of the labels generated by our algorithm was measured against the truth. We report our accuracy of phase contour labeling for both cases - labels present within the phase diagram (94%) and labels that have to be inferred (88%).

We believe that the results show promise, as seen in Figs. 6 and 3. Our contour extraction and text classification works well even for varied contour sizes and shapes. A minimalistic demo application constructed using our methods is shown in Figs. 7(a) and (b), where we display the transformed physical coordinates as well as the phase of the material at the cursor position.

14   B. Urala Kota et al.

Discovery of Bulk Metallic-Glasses

Aside from the phase information, we also detect 'eutectic points' (see Sect. 1), which are point(s) in a phase diagram indicating the chemical composition and temperature corresponding to the lowest melting point of a mixture of components. These points serve as an important first order signature of alloy chemistries and are vital for design of 'metallic-glasses', a class of material of increasing interest and importance. The eutectic points can be determined by analyzing the smoothened contour of the liquid phase, for which both contour separation and accurate matching of label and region is critical. We also measure the so-called 'eutectic angle' corresponding to each eutectic point which is defined as the angle formed by the contour lines leading into and out of the eutectic point. An example is seen in Fig. 8. Blue circles are used to mark the location of eutectic points and the corresponding angles are shown nearby.

We analyzed a database of binary metallic phase diagrams and quantitatively defined that a deep eutectic angle is roughly between 0° and 75°. This value was defined by identifying the design rule which most correctly identified metallic glass forming compounds. This work therefore allows us to define the 'deep eutectic' in terms of a design rule, as opposed to the more general usage of the term to date. When combined with radii difference scaled by composition (the value along the X-axis) at the eutectic point, we were able to identify binary metallic systems that were likely to form metallic glasses. Following this analysis, we identified 6 different binary metallic systems to have a *high probability* of metallic-glass formation, which were previously unknown. A complete list of 38 different systems, with exact compositions and temperatures, which were previously unidentified as glass-forming, uncovered due to our work, are listed in [4].

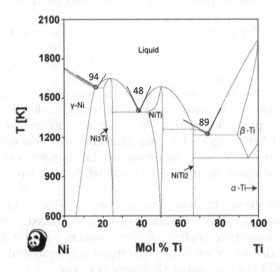

Fig. 8. Detection of eutectic points and angles in phase diagrams. Best viewed in color. (Color figure online)

Conclusion

Given the importance of a digitized phase diagram database to the materials community at large, we believe that our effort in developing automated tools to digitize phase diagrams from technical papers is a valuable contribution with significant impact. In the future, we would like to create a comprehensive, high resolution database of phase diagrams, and improve label and phase region matching tasks. We would also like to extend our work to support the detection and storage of critical points and material parameters which are key in design and manufacture of certain materials. Further, the materials domain is rich in graphs, figures and tables that contain valuable information, which when combined and collated into large indexable, digital databases, would help the materials community to accelerate the discovery of new and exciting materials.

Acknowledgments. This material is based upon work supported by the National Science Foundation under Grant No.1640867 (OAC/DMR). Any opinions, findings, and conclusions or recommendations expressed in this material are those of the author(s) and do not necessarily reflect the views of the National Science Foundation.

References

1. Elzer, S., Carberry, S., Zukerman, I.: The automated understanding of simple bar charts. Artif. Intell. **175**(2), 526–555 (2011)
2. Carberry, S., Elzer, S., Demir, S.: Information graphics: an untapped resource for digital libraries. In: Proceedings of the 29th Annual International ACM SIGIR Conference on Research and Development in Information Retrieval, pp. 581–588. ACM (2006)
3. Lu, X., Kataria, S., Brouwer, W.J., Wang, J.Z., Mitra, P., Giles, C.L.: Automated analysis of images in documents for intelligent document search. IJDAR **12**, 65–81 (2009)
4. Dasgupta, A., et al.: Probabilistic assessment of glass forming ability rules for metallic glasses aided by automated analysis of phase diagrams. Scientific Reports - under review (2018)
5. Blostein, D., Lank, E., Zanibbi, R.: Treatment of diagrams in document image analysis. In: Anderson, M., Cheng, P., Haarslev, V. (eds.) Diagrams 2000. LNCS (LNAI), vol. 1889, pp. 330–344. Springer, Heidelberg (2000). https://doi.org/10.1007/3-540-44590-0_29
6. Shahab, A., Shafait, F., Dengel, A.: ICDAR 2011 robust reading competition challenge 2: reading text in scene images. In: International Conference on Document Analysis and Recognition (2011)
7. Zhou, Y.P., Tan, C.L.: Bar charts recognition using hough based syntactic segmentation. In: Anderson, M., Cheng, P., Haarslev, V. (eds.) Diagrams 2000. LNCS (LNAI), vol. 1889, pp. 494–497. Springer, Heidelberg (2000). https://doi.org/10.1007/3-540-44590-0_45
8. Nair, R.R., Sankaran, N., Nwogu, I., Govindaraju, V.: Automated analysis of line plots in documents. In: 2015 13th International Conference on Document Analysis and Recognition (ICDAR), pp. 796–800. IEEE (2015)
9. Radhakrishnan Nair, R., Sankaran, N., Nwogu, I., Govindaraju, V.: Understanding line plots using bayesian network. In: 2016 12th IAPR Workshop on Document Analysis Systems (DAS), pp. 108–113. IEEE (2016)

10. Rege, P.P., Chandrakar, C.A.: Text-image separation in document images using boundary/perimeter detection. ACEEE Int. J. Sig. Image Process. **3**(1), 10–14 (2012)
11. Mishchenko, A., Vassilieva, N.: Chart image understanding and numerical data extraction. In: Sixth International Conference on Digital Information Management (ICDIM) (2011)
12. Duda, R.O., Hart, P.E.: Use of the hough transformation to detect lines and curves in pictures. Commun. ACM **15**(1), 11–15 (1972)
13. Smith, R.: An overview of the tesseract OCR engine. In: ICDAR, vol. 7, pp. 629–633 (2007)
14. Choudhury, P.S., Wang, S., Giles, L.: Automated data extraction from scholarly line graphs. In: GREC (2015)
15. Elzer, S., Carberry, S., Demir, S.: Communicative signals as the key to automated understanding of simple bar charts. In: Barker-Plummer, D., Cox, R., Swoboda, N. (eds.) Diagrams 2006. LNCS (LNAI), vol. 4045, pp. 25–39. Springer, Heidelberg (2006). https://doi.org/10.1007/11783183_5
16. Perrault, C.R., Allen, J.F.: A plan-based analysis of indirect speech acts. Comput. Linguist. **6**(3–4), 167–182 (1980)
17. Campbell, F.C.: Phase Diagrams: Understanding the Basics. ASM International (2012)
18. Computational phase diagram database. cpddb.nims.go.jp/cpddb/periodic.htm. Accessed 06 Feb 2017
19. Otsu, N.: A threshold selection method from gray-level histograms. Automatica **11**(285–296), 23–27 (1975)
20. Suzuki, S., et al.: Topological structural analysis of digitized binary images by border following. Comput. Vis. Graph. Image Process. **30**(1), 32–46 (1985)
21. Hu, M.K.: Visual pattern recognition by moment invariants. IRE Trans. Inf. Theory **8**(2), 179–187 (1962)
22. Flusser, J., Suk, T.: Rotation moment invariants for recognition of symmetric objects. IEEE Trans. Image Process. **15**(12), 3784–3790 (2006)
23. Zhang, Y., Wang, S., Sun, P., Phillips, P.: Pathological brain detection based on wavelet entropy and hu moment invariants. Bio-med. Mater. Eng. **26**(s1), S1283–S1290 (2015)
24. Russell, B.C., Torralba, A., Murphy, K.P., Freeman, W.T.: LabelMe: a database and web-based tool for image annotation. Int. J. Comput. Vis. **77**(1), 157–173 (2008)

An Approach for Detecting Circular Callouts in Architectural, Engineering and Constructional Drawing Documents

Sandip Kumar Maity[1], Bhagesh Seraogi[1], Supriya Das[1],
Purnendu Banerjee[1(✉)], Himadri Majumder[1], Srinivas Mukkamala[1],
Rahul Roy[1], and Bidyut B. Chaudhuri[2]

[1] ARC Document Solutions, Kolkata, India
{sandip.maity,bhagesh.seraogi,supriya.das,
purnendu.banerjee,himadri.majumder,
srinivas.mukkamala,rahul.roy}@e-arc.com
[2] Indian Statistical Institute, CVPR Unit, Kolkata, India
bbcisical@gmail.com

Abstract. A set of documents, while creating a building structure, containing the fundamental assumptions and the primary requirements are called engineering construction documents. It acts as a blueprint to provide the engineers or architects a bird's-eye view of the whole project. Generally, an engineering project comprises of large number of document sheets. These sheets maintain the constructional hierarchy of the projects. Accessing the information manually from a desired sheet becomes laborious and time consuming for an engineer or architect. Therefore, a hyperlinked navigation mechanism is essential to overcome the aforesaid problem. A special graphical representation named 'callout', which is usually circular in shape, contains the destination sheet names in such documents. In the automated project navigation process, a callout with the respective destination sheet name must be recognized properly. The destination sheet names are written in an abbreviated form in the callout. Here, we have proposed a novel software approach which can detect the circular callouts and also create hyperlinks to the destination sheets. This work has a significant impact in the AEC (Architectural, Engineering, Constructional) domain and we achieved very encouraging results by our method.

Keywords: AEC drawing documents · Callouts · Circle detection
Text localization

1 Introduction

Engineers or architects develop their drawings using the combination of several graphical representations, i.e. symbols, line-segments, circles, circular arcs, etc. Such drawing documents are widely used in Architectural, Constructional and Engineering (AEC) domain. The amount of data, AEC industry handles is enormous and manipulation process of these documents is a challenging task. Still several of these processes involve manual interventions. Hence, the whole process of data retrieval from AEC

A. Fornés and B. Lamiroy (Eds.): GREC 2017, LNCS 11009, pp. 17–29, 2018.
https://doi.org/10.1007/978-3-030-02284-6_2

documents becomes very time consuming and error prone. Also, the presence of graphics makes things even more complicated. Furthermore, the difficulty in accurate text extraction increases due to different orientation in graphical shapes. As the AEC industry deals with huge number of documents for a project, it is necessary to use several sheets for depicting the desired information and some symbolic way of referring from one document to the other. One such symbolic representation is called "callout". The overall appearance of a callout is normally circular, which have several other structural properties. Some examples of callouts are shown in the Fig. 1. The callout contains some text which represents other document sheet name and section number. In an AEC project, it is cumbersome to navigate through all the documents of a project. One document may refer to several other for various purposes. Thus, automatic callout detection and sheet number extraction play helpful role for engineers working with them.

Fig. 1. Examples of various type of callouts (including handwritten).

In this paper, we have proposed one approach which can automatically detect the callouts in AEC drawing documents and recognize the document sheet number successfully. This approach can also be applied for the detection of other circular symbolic representations in other drawing documents with some modifications. In Fig. 2, the presence of callouts with orientation variation is shown.

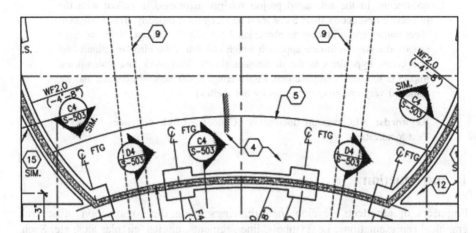

Fig. 2. A cropped region of an AEC drawing document consisting of callouts

1.1 Related Work

In the literature, there exists several works [11–18] which can detect circular shapes. Among them [16–18] are based on Hough transform. However, those are computationally expensive, and do not provide sufficient accuracy in the localization of the center and end points of the detected arcs. In [11], Kim et al. proposed a two-step circle detection method. In the first step they detected the center based on Hough transform and in second step they tried to detect radii by radius histogram. In [12], Xiaoyu used scan line based RANSAC algorithm to detect circular shapes. De et al. present a method in [13] to recognize and classify graphics in engineering drawings by skeletonizing the input image, followed by segmentation of lines, arcs, and circles. Extracted line segments are classified into object lines, centerlines, dashed lines, section lines and arcs. The stages of segmentation and classification are based on dominant chain. In [14], Dosch et al. proposed a method which works on chains of points, or on segments obtained by the polygonal approximation of such chains. The basic idea is to compute an estimation of the curvature for these chains. They suggested a vectorization process where the pixels of the skeleton are linked together to form chains, and a polygonal approximation converted the chains into straight line segments. Bart Lamiroy et al. presents a method in [15] for detecting circular shapes, which is also based on RANSAC algorithm.

The primary challenge here is the symbol recognition [19], in which an automatic way is sought to identify various special constructs in the floor plan such as doors and windows. Several researchers have investigated the problem and reported impressive results. Most existing algorithms focused solely on the symbol recognition [20] and did not provide a complete solution for the reconstruction problem.

Most of the existing text/graphic separation methods [3–8] can be categorized into three approaches: 1st approach: Extract text first, leaving non-text objects behind [6, 8]; 2nd approach: Extract non-text elements first, leaving text behind [10]; and the 3rd approach: Recognize both text and graphical objects at the same time based on their discriminative characteristics [3].

In a document, the callouts containing texts, can be oriented in any direction (Fig. 2). Hence, existing text localization methods [9, 10] may fail to detect the callout texts. In [9] Chowdhury et al. used a morphological operation to detect graphics and line arts and finally extracted the texts.

But AEC class of drawing documents are mixture of symbols, texts, and graphics. So, callout like symbol detection and text extraction from it is a difficult task. The callouts are not perfect circles. It contains of several other features. Therefore, additional care should be taken for detecting them. The description of our proposed method, results and discussion, conclusion and future scope are described in Sects. 2, 3 and 4, respectively.

2 Proposed Method

The overall workflow of our proposed method is briefly given below:

I. A preprocessing step is applied to create a binarized image of smaller dpi (dots per inch).

II. Then we apply a graphics removal process to enrich the document with relevant information.

III. Now, a text block localization method is executed where each component is labelled, and grouping done for the components of similar pattern.

IV. Next a circle detection method is applied on the text block localized region.

V. To identify the exact location of the document sheet name, first the mid-line (the mid-line is the line separating the circle into two nearby equal halves.) of the circle is detected, and then the desired document sheet name is extracted.

VI. Finally, the detected text portion is recognized by a custom-built OCR (Optical Character Recognition) engine and the text is auto hyperlinked to the desired document sheet name.

2.1 Preprocessing

Documents created in AEC industry are very big in size. Therefore, handling such document is difficult. But, all the foreground pixels present in the image may not be of much use while recognizing or detecting text or graphical objects. Hence, first we do reduce the size in half of the original image. Then this reduced gray image is binarized.

2.2 Graphics Removal

AEC documents contain several types of line and textual patterns. A Connected Component Labelling (CCL) technique is used to get the shape and size information. We remove the large sized graphical/non-textual components obtained by CCL technique. In drawing documents, the line patterns, e.g., dashed lines, dotted lines etc., which have similar textual structural properties, should also be removed. Therefore, we have applied a noise removal technique. From the component set, three components are recursively and consecutively selected to form several groups. Now, for each component of a group, the center point is calculated and checked for co-linearity among themselves. If the group count surpasses a heuristically learned threshold, maintaining the co-linearity, then those groups are removed from the component set and the remaining components are retained. In (Fig. 3b) it can be seen that the majority of the line patterns (assumed as noise for our problem) are removed efficiently. It will make the input image text rich. The main problem here is, characters or parts of them, especially in their extraordinary large or small sizes, exhibit similar shape characteristics as non-text graphical objects, which will confuse the recognition of the latter.

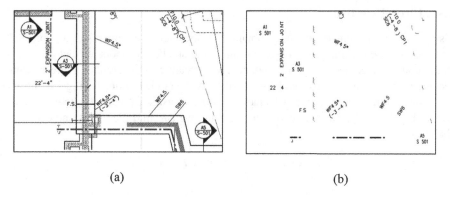

(a)   (b)

Fig. 3. (a) Cropped image of a drawing documents (b) Initial grouping (line pattern and graphical objects are removed)

2.3 Text Block Localization

After removing sufficient amount of large graphical objects and noise pixels, therefore, the next objective is to localize the text block regions. To fulfil our aim, we need to cluster the components and form the text blocks. Now, on the remaining components set, a grouping approach is applied based on the distance between two components and their overlapping area in a set. While grouping, we have searched in all the directions from the center point of each component to make our method orientation independent. Finally, a region of text is localized and set as region of interest, i.e., ROI (Fig. 4b). Now, this ROI is used to initiate the callout detection mechanism.

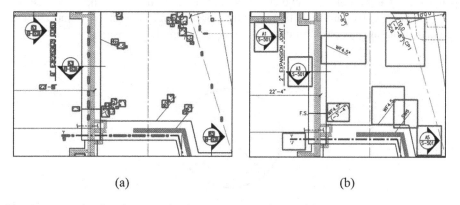

(a)   (b)

Fig. 4. (a) Red colored rectangular boxes represent the candidate text blocks (b) Localized regions of text components (Color figure online)

2.4 Circle Detection

Using the original binarized image obtained in the preprocessing stage, a connected component-based technique is used to remove the smaller components and retain the larger components (see Fig. 5b). Now, positional features and size-based thresholding technique is used on the inverted image to identify the circle region. Taking 4 points by traversing from four sides we get black to white transition points. If these 4 points satisfy Eq. 1 and then it is treated as a circle and we can find the radius and center of the circle.

$$X^2 + Y^2 + AX + BY + C = 0 \tag{1}$$

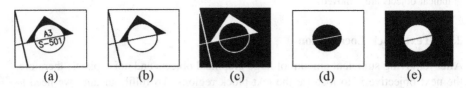

Fig. 5. (a) Candidate callout (b) After the removal of textual components (c) Negative Image (d) Contour area and (e) Middle line extraction

Then we exploit a geometrical property for the validation of the circles. If we draw two chords, i.e. $\overline{AC}$ and $\overline{CE}$ by using three consecutive points, lying on the circumference of that circle, then the perpendiculars (i.e. $\overline{BG}$ and $\overline{DH}$) drawn from the mid points (i.e., B and D) of those two chords will intersect each other at the center (i.e. F) of the circle (Fig. 6). This condition stays true for any three consecutive points and the perpendiculars always pass through the center of the circle.

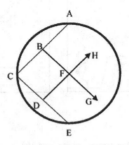

Fig. 6. Geometrical property of a circle

2.5   Middle Line Detection

Generally, a straight line passes through the center of a callout. This is one of the primary features of a circular callout. This line can also be treated as the diameter of the callout. Now a Hough transformed-based line detection method [18] is used to extract the lines from the edge image. The middle line or diameter of the circle is detected by calculating perpendicular distance from the center of the image. The minimum distance among those distances containing line is the diameter of the circle. In our algorithm, middle line plays a major role. It helps us to separate the top and bottom portion of the callouts. It is also used for orientation detection of the callouts. After the detection of proper orientation, the middle line is removed. While experimenting, we have noted that the portion, which contains maximum number of components, represents the destination sheet number. Thus, the appropriate sheet number containing region is extracted.

2.6   Text Extraction

Text extraction from the circular callouts is also a challenging task. At first, the sheet number region is restored from the original image and then it is binarized using a standard thresholding technique. Now, we drop a perpendicular (Fig. 7) from each pixel present on the mid-line in the vertical direction and store the distance at which the perpendicular first hits a data pixel. Then, by analyzing the distance curve we try to identify the rate of change of the gradient (Fig. 8) for both sides of the bilateral symmetric curve. For each of the extracted half circle, the gradient change is considered as positive for the left region and negative for the right region. We have exploited this observation to eliminate the unwanted segment of the circle. Now, we try to identify a position where the aforementioned behavior of the gradient fails. In Fig. 8, point A and B are the two segmentation points. Finally, the left portion of point A and right portion of point B are eliminated from the half circle and get more precise location of the text regions.

Now, while analyzing the connected component labels, we take the center of each component and align them in the horizontal direction. Then we try to identify the outlier which lies at the maximum distance from each of the centers and finally remove it. This approach is applied such that we can maximize the accurate extraction of the text regions in case of a touching or noisy callout.

Fig. 7. Pictorial representation of vertical scan line mechanism

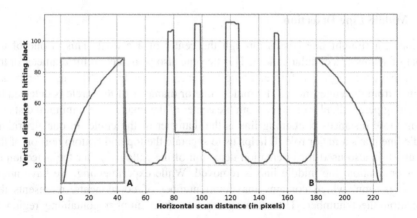

Fig. 8. Graphical representation of vertically downwards scanline distances

2.7 Text Recognition

Text recognition is vital in any document analysis and retrieval system [21–23]. In case of drawing documents, the texts inside the callout represent information about other documents. These texts are generally machine printed (in some cases handwritten callouts are also found). Also, the presence of noise and overlapping text region makes it difficult for the conventional OCR systems to accurately recognize the texts. Therefore, we have developed a full-fledged OCR engine where Support Vector Machine (SVM) is used as a classifier. For feature extraction 3 sets of features are used, i.e. (a) 28 features based on distance from four boundary points (each of the 4 sides of the bounding box of the image is divided into 7 bins, making a total 28 bins, Fig. 9(a)), (b) 8-directional feature from center point to outer boundary of the character component (Fig. 9(b)) and (c) 16 features block representation (whole image is equally divided into 16 blocks, Fig. 9(c)). Therefore, in total 52 features are used for the classification task. Then, all the detected callout images are fed to the OCR engine which also utilizes some of the features mentioned in [21–23]. Here, in total 64 classes are considered including all upper and lower-case characters, numerical digits and two special symbols i.e. {'.', '-'}. So total 64 classes. We have used 250 data per class for training.

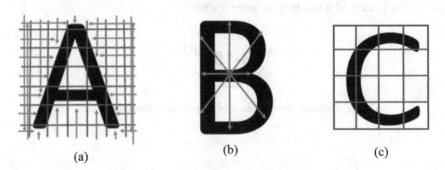

(a)   (b)   (c)

Fig. 9. Pictorial representation of various features (a) Scan line mechanism from boundary of bounding box to character body (b) 8 directional distance from center of the image to outer boundary in 45° interval (c) Block based feature

3   Results and Discussion

The method has been experimented on a fairly large dataset, consisting of several categories of AEC class of documents. We have tested our method on a dataset containing 1320 data images. These images are gathered from different architects to train and test different callout patterns. We have achieved callout detection accuracy of 96.72%, which is quite satisfactory given the complexity and variety of callouts. While experimenting on the AEC data set, we have noted that our OCR engine achieves better accuracy with respect to the Tesseract OCR. The comparison of accuracy is shown in Table 2.

The text localization and text recognition accuracy are 94.68% and 98.53% respectively (see Table 1). Due to the presence of noise and overlapping of text with graphics, it becomes difficult to localize and recognize the text properly. In Table 3, the intermediate results of sheet number extraction from various callout images are shown. Our proposed method not only extract the destination sheet number from an ideal and clean callout image, but also it is robust enough to handle complex (including handwritten callouts) and noisy callout images. In Table 3, we have shown how our approach can successfully handle such noisy images. Also, one sample output of the finally hyperlinked destination sheet names is presented in Fig. 10.

Table 1. Stages and their accuracies

Process	Accuracy (%)
Text localization	94.68
Callout detection	96.72
Text recognition	98.53
End-to-end performance	90.22

Table 2. OCR accuracy

OCR	Accuracy (%)
Tesseract	95.19
In-house OCR	98.53

Table 3. Intermediate results of sheet number extraction method (The last row is hand-drawn callout)

Sample callout regions	Middle line removal	Orientation correction and ROI for sheet name extraction	Circle segment removal on both sides	Finally extracted text region	OCRed result
					S-109
					S-501
					S-503
					S-530B
					S-520B
					S-101C

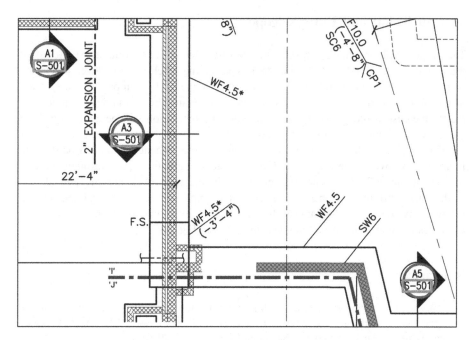

Fig. 10. Final results are shown in the cropped sample image

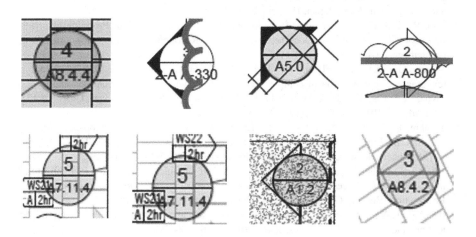

Fig. 11. Callout images with different category of noise

4 Conclusion and Future Scope

The proposed algorithmic approach can efficiently detect the callouts in AEC class of drawing documents. Also, the callout text hyperlinking mechanism is developed based on the work proposed in [1, 2] and used to automate the navigation process. Integration of this approach software to any commercial systems in AEC domain will immensely reduce the cost of navigation time. Also, manual intervention will be almost removed while hyperlinking the destination sheet names.

Though this method gives promising results, a few enhancements can be done in future to improve its performance. Cases where straight lines pass through the text regions of the callouts or the characters within the text block are overlapped, our method may produce erroneous results. After employing line removal mechanism followed by an in-painting approach may help to overcome such situations. Some examples of such difficult callouts are given in the Fig. 11.

References

1. Banerjee, P., Choudhary, S., Das, S., Majumdar, H., Roy, R., Chaudhuri, B.B.: Automatic hyperlinking of engineering drawing documents. In: Proceedings of 12th IAPR Workshop on Document Analysis Systems, Santorini, Greece, (April 2016)
2. Banerjee, P., et al.: A system for automatic navigation in architectural and construction documents. In: Proceedings of 14th IAPR International Conference on Document Analysis and Recognition, Kyto, Japan, (November 2017)
3. Cao, R., Tan, C.L.: Separation of overlapping text from graphics. In: Proceedings of 6th International Conference on Document Analysis and Recognition, Seattle, USA, pp. 44–48, (September 2001)
4. Moreno-García, C.F., Elyan, E., Jayne, C.: Heuristics-based detection to improve text/graphics segmentation in complex engineering drawings. In: Boracchi, G., Iliadis, L., Jayne, C., Likas, A. (eds.) EANN 2017. CCIS, vol. 744, pp. 87–98. Springer, Cham (2017). https://doi.org/10.1007/978-3-319-65172-9_8
5. Tombre, K., Tabbone, S., Pélissier, L., Lamiroy, B., Dosch, P.: Text/graphics separation revisited. In: Lopresti, D., Hu, J., Kashi, R. (eds.) DAS 2002. LNCS, vol. 2423, pp. 200–211. Springer, Heidelberg (2002). https://doi.org/10.1007/3-540-45869-7_24
6. Ahmed, S., Weber, M., Liwicki, M., Dengel, A.: Text_graphics segmentation in architectural floor plans. In: Proceedings of International Conference on Document Analysis and Recognition, Beijing, China, pp. 1520–5363/11, (September 20011)
7. Fletcher, L.A., Kasturi, R.: A robust algorithm for text string separation from mixed text/graphics images. IEEE Trans. PAMI **10**(6), 910–918 (1988)
8. Chowdhury, S.P., Mandal, S., Das, A.K., Chanda, B.: Segmentation of text and graphics from document images. In: Proceedings of the International Conference on Document Analysis and Recognition, 2 (Section 4), pp. 619–623 (2007)
9. Lu, Z.: Detection of text regions from digital engineering drawings. IEEE Trans. PAMI **20**(4), 431–439 (1998)
10. Hoang, T.V., Tabbone, S.: Text extraction from graphical document images using sparse representation. In: Proceedings of 9th IAPR Workshop on Document Analysis Systems, Boston, USA, pp. 143–150, (June 2010)

11. Kim, H.S., Kim, J.H.: A two-step circle detection algorithm from the intersecting chords. In: Proceedings of International Conference on Robotics and Biomimetics (ICRB), pp. 787–798, April 2001. Patt. Recogn. Lett. **22**(6/7)
12. Xiaoyu, S., Ting, J., Shuai, Y., Song, G., Yuxin, L.: Scanning line based random sample consensus algorithm for fast arc detection. In: Proceedings of International Conference on Robotics and Biomimetics, Qingdao, China, pp. 1117–1122, (December 2016)
13. De, P., Mandal, S., Das, A., Bhowmick, P.: A new approach to detect and classify graphic primitives in engineering drawings. In: Proceedings of 4th International Conference of Emerging Applications of Information Technology, Kolkata, India, pp. 243–248 (2014)
14. Dosch, P., Masini, G., Tombre, K.: Improving arc detection in graphics recognition. In: Proceedings of 15th International Conference on Pattern Recognition, (September 2000)
15. Lamiroy, B., Guebbas, Y.: Robust and precise circular arc detection. In: Ogier, J.-M., Liu, W., Lladós, J. (eds.) GREC 2009. LNCS, vol. 6020, pp. 49–60. Springer, Heidelberg (2010). https://doi.org/10.1007/978-3-642-13728-0_5
16. Ye, H., Shang, G., Wang, L., Zheng, M.: A new method based on Hough Transform for quick line and circle detection. In: Proceedings of 8th International Conference on BioMedical Engineering and Informatics, Shenyang, China, pp. 52–56 (2015)
17. Rizon, M., et al.: Object detection using circular hough transform. Am. J. Appl. Sci. **2**(12), 1606–1609 (2005)
18. Duda, R.O., Hart, P.E.: Use of the hough transformation to detect lines and curves pictures. Commun. ACM **15**(1), 11–15 (1972)
19. Banerjee, P., Chaudhuri, B.B.: An approach for bangla and devanagari video text recognition. In: Proceedings of International Workshop on Multilingual OCR (MOCR), Washington DC, USA (2013). Article no. 8
20. Cordella, L.P., Vento, M.: Symbol recognition in documents: a collection of techniques. Int. J. Doc. Image Anal. **3**(2), 73–88 (2000)
21. Banerjee, P., Chaudhuri, B.B.: An approach for Bangla and devanagari video text. In: Proceedings of International Workshop on Multilingual OCR, Washington DC, USA
22. Tripathy, N., Chakraborti, T., Nasipuri, M., Pal, U.: A scale and rotation invariant scheme for multi-oriented character recognition. In: Proceedings of International Conference on Pattern Recognition, pp. 4041–4046, (December 2016)
23. Banerjee, P., Bhowmick, S.: Bangla text recognition from video sequence: a new focus. In: Proceedings of 2nd National Conference on Computing and Systems, pp. 62–67, (March 2012)

A System for Automatic Elevation Datum Detection and Hyperlinking of AEC Drawing Documents

Purnendu Banerjee[1]($\boxtimes$), Supriya Das[1], Bhagesh Seraogi[1],
Himadri Majumder[1], Srinivas Mukkamala[1], Rahul Roy[1],
and Bidyut B. Chaudhuri[2]

[1] ARC Document Solutions, Kolkata, India
{purnendu.banerjee,supriya.das,bhagesh.seraogi,
himadri.majumder,srinivas.mukkamala,
rahul.roy}@e-arc.com
[2] Indian Statistical Institute, CVPR Unit, Kolkata, India
bbcisical@gmail.com

Abstract. In AEC (Architecture, Engineering & Construction) industry, drawing documents are used as a blueprint to facilitate the construction process. It also acts as a graphical language that helps to communicate ideas and information from one mind to another. A construction project generally contains huge number of such drawing documents. An engineer or architect often needs to refer various documents while creating a new one or marking irregularities in such documents. Elevation datum is one of such graphical representation medium for referring one document from another. It is a very difficult and time-consuming task to manually identify elevation datums and link the documents with respect to each datum. Here, our proposed method is aimed to overcome this hurdle. The suggested system will automatically find the elevation datums from the existing drawing documents and will also automate the hyperlinking mechanism to enable the engineer quickly navigate among different drawing files. We have achieved an overall accuracy of 96.71% for elevation datum detection and destination document text recognition on a fairly large sized database.

Keywords: AEC drawing documents · Automatic hyperlinking
Elevation datum · Circular hough transform · OCR · SVM classifier

1 Introduction

An AEC project requires blueprint or plan documents before starting the work on the ground. A sample of AEC drawing document is shown in the Fig. 1. An engineering drawing is a type of technical drawing, used to fully and clearly define the requirements for engineering and manufacturing items, and is usually created in accordance with standardized conventions of layout, nomenclature, interpretation, appearance size etc. Its purpose is to unambiguously capture all the geometric features of a product or component. A construction work involves different categories of skilled individuals

© Springer Nature Switzerland AG 2018
A. Fornés and B. Lamiroy (Eds.): GREC 2017, LNCS 11009, pp. 30–42, 2018.
https://doi.org/10.1007/978-3-030-02284-6_3

such as Engineers, Architects, Electricians, Contractor, Plumbers etc. For different tasks, the AEC drawing documents make it possible to quickly understand the whole project. For a project, the documents are usually inter-related, and the engineers often refers to different documents while preparing a new one or detecting irregularities at any project site.

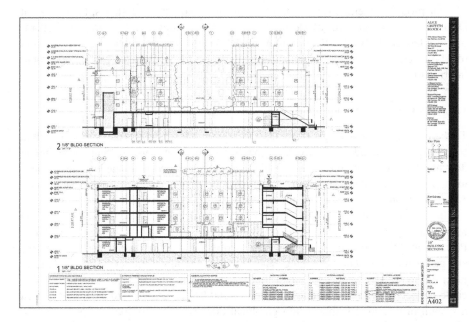

Fig. 1. An example of AEC drawing document.

AEC projects involve a huge number of documents and one document may refer to another document. Therefore, manual navigation from one document to another is very difficult and a time-consuming task. Moreover, if the drawing sheets are not properly indexed, then this process becomes even more problematic. In that case the engineers or architects must visit each document in order to identify whether the destination documents are correctly referred or not. As a solution, by creating hyperlinks in these drawing documents, the navigation mechanism can be given a very significant boost. To achieve this goal, we require the destination document and the accurate path of this document. Then only this manual intervention of the navigation process can be removed by creating an indexing based automated system. In this paper, we proposed such a system which will automatically locate the destination file by extracting its name from the referring document sheet and finally creating the hyperlink.

In AEC class of drawing documents, the linking information is represented by a circular shape drawn on the desired portion in the document sheet. Such a shape is commonly called as 'Callout'. Another popular representation of linking information is denoted by 'Elevation Datum (ED)'. ED is also circular in shape, but a horizontal and a vertical line crossing through the center divides the circle into four parts as Top-Left,

Top-Right, Bottom-Left, Bottom-Right. The major graphical property of ED is that the diagonally opposite quarters (see Fig. 2) of the ED is always filled with the same colour, i.e. white or black. Also, a horizontally or vertically drawn dash-line (also called Sectional line) is used for referring the destination document name as text. Depending on the architects or engineers, this text appears either at the top of the dash-line or at the bottom.

Our proposed method can be divided into the following four stages, (a) Elevation Datum location detection, (b) Destination Text localization and text-graphics separation, (c) Optical Character Recognition (OCR) of localized destination text region and (d) Hyperlinking of the destination sheet with respect to the extracted linking document information.

1.1   Background

To the best of our knowledge, there is no existing work which has tackled the problem stated above. Though there exists some literature where engineering or technical drawing documents are processed, yet they are not equipped with adequate techniques to tackle our problem However, some closely related literatures are cited here. A common problem of any symbol processing systems, recognition or spotting, is localization or detection of the symbols. The method may be embedded in the recognition/spotting method or work as a separated stage in a two-stage system [8]. Pham et al. [9] proposed an approach for symbol localization using junction features and geometry consistency checking. They used to find three different types of T, L, X junction point. They also mentioned that their system will fail to detect symbol like circle connected with line, due to omission of end key point. Do et al. [10] represented a system of detecting symbols into graphical documents using sparse representation. More specifically, a dictionary is learned from a training database of local descriptors defined over the documents. In our method there is no need of supervised learning to detect the ED.

Banerjee et al. [1] have used a Hough transform based approach for detecting the callouts in engineering drawing documents and finally hyperlinked them. Najman et al. [2] have worked on locating the tittle block in engineering drawings. In [4], the authors have worked on automatic detection of version information in computer-aided design and drafting (CADD) Drawings using engineering drawing interpretation. They have proposed a knowledge-based version information extraction method which analyzes the layout of the drawing frame and extracts the version information with the help of predefined key words. Z. Lu et al. have proposed a method for detecting text regions from digital engineering drawings in [5]. Therefore, to the best of our knowledge, no previous work for automatic detection of ED in AEC class of drawing documents exist. Automatic ED detection is a new work in this domain.

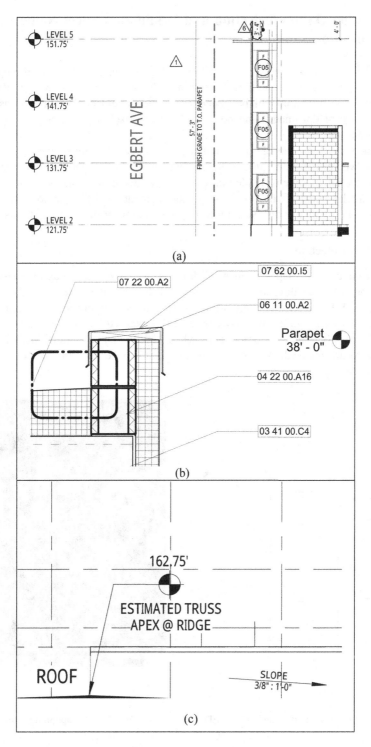

Fig. 2. Different types of ED representations. The desired texts may appear on the right (a)/left (b)/top or bottom(c) side of an ED.

2 Elevation Datum Detection and Destination Sheet Name Localization

The AEC class of documents are generally very big in size. Therefore, handling such a document is quite difficult and time consuming. The higher the dpi of a document will be, the more information will be generated in the document. We have considered different range of dpi images and noted that our approach achieves a good accuracy with 300 dpi images.

We mentioned that the EDs are circular in shape and they are segmented into four quadrants where opposite quadrants are similar in their graphical representation. Our ED detection module is divided into two stages. In the first stage we have detected the near circular shapes. In the second stage, the segregation of ED and non-ED circular shapes is done by analyzing the graphical representation of the four quadrants.

2.1 Circle Detection

To detect the circular shapes in an AEC drawing, we have used Hough transform [3] based approach. The threshold parameters of HT are learned heuristically. Before applying the HT, we have converted the image into an edge image using canny edge detector. This step significantly reduces the time required by HT in order to detect circles. Thus, only boundary components (which signify that less amount of foreground information) are retained. An example of the input image and corresponding canny output image is presented in Fig. 3.

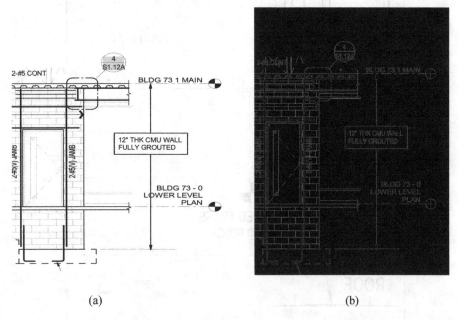

(a)   (b)

Fig. 3. (a) Original input image where ED notation is used, (b) Corresponding Canny edge image.

We can represent a circle in two-dimensional space, where parameters will represent center and radius of the circle, respectively. Generally, architects follow a standard notation while creating a circular shaped ED. But, in some cases we have seen that the ED size varies. That is why we have considered a radius range for detecting the circles from the documents. For each point on the candidate image, a circle can be defined with a center residing at point (x, y) having radius, say, r. The intersection point of all such candidate circles in the parameter space corresponds to the center point of the original circle.

Due to the use of HT more than one circle may get detected with a single circle center point. To solve this problem, we have heuristically learned the parameter values of HT, e.g. Minimum Radius, Maximum Radius, Voting Threshold for Center and Minimum Distance between two center points. Since ED is not exactly circular in shape, therefore we have experimented with different values of the voting parameter/ center threshold to detect as many ED as possible. Table 1 shows the corresponding accuracy performance test of true ED circle detection by tuning the center threshold. Here, we have noted that, when the center threshold is decreased, the circle detection rate increases. But, it also increases the false circle detection rate. So, we have enabled our approach with a mechanism which can identify the false circles and then they are discarded.

Table 1. Circle detection accuracy by changing the center threshold

Center voting threshold	Number of file tested	Number of true circle present	Number of true circle detected	True circle accuracy
85	1040	12446	9847	79.12
65	1040	12446	10649	85.56
55	1040	12446	11005	88.42
45	1040	12446	11518	92.54
25	**1040**	**12446**	**12309**	**98.90**
15	1040	12446	12315	98.01

Since the shape is not perfectly circle, you can shift the center within a small region and collect all the votes for each center position and assume that they lie in the same "near circle" shape. You can give tolerance in the radius too. It may increase false detection of circle, but in a false circle if you pick some random points on the perimeter, and see their neighborhood lines, then those lines may not be circular shaped. If that happens, you can discard the detected circle.

From the experimental results, it is quite clear that we achieve the highest accuracy at the center threshold of 25. We tested with different architect documents. We can see merely decreasing the center threshold does not help us to increase our final ED detection accuracy, since the false circle detection rate also increases. Now, our goal is to identify the proper ED shape.

2.2   Elevation Datum Detection

We have already stated that ED notations are nearly circular, and they are divided into four equal parts where the diagonally opposite parts contain white or black colour. Figure 4 shows two types of ED notations.

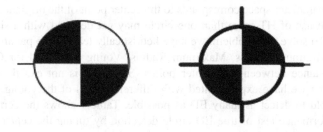

Fig. 4. Different types of elevation Datum notation.

Now, we generate the contour of each circle which was earlier detected by our circle detection module in Fig. 5a shows different circle detected by circle detection module. There has some false circle is present which not represent ED. In the next stage we removed false circle using contour analysis. Figure 5b represent different contours in green, orange colour within the circle. Then, we find which circle contains four almost equal sized contours and then check the pixel intensities of each contour. Now, if it is found that the diagonally opposite contours are filled with the same colour component, then that circle is tagged as an elevation datum circle. Finally, all the circles validating the aforesaid property are considered as ED in Fig. 5c.

2.3   Destination Sheet Name Localization

After the detection of ED, we need to find the destination sheet name associated with each ED. The destination sheet name generally appears on the right side or left side of the datum. Therefore, at first, the sectional line's positional appearance which is associated with a datum, is to be found. To achieve this, Hough line detection algorithm is applied on the pre-processed image.

After detecting the sectional line (see Fig. 7), we try to find the associated text region near the sectional line region. The sheet name may be printed in single or multi line format. In Fig. 5, the sheet name is in multi-line format. So, at-first we try to locate the position of the text region with respect to the sectional line. Initially, we separate the image horizontally in two halves with respect to the sectional line. While experimenting, it is noted that the height of the destination sheet name component is always less than the diameter length of the ED. Also, we have used the value of the diameter as the vertical distance (with respect to the sectional line), within which the document name should appear. Now, a connected component labelling based approach is applied to spot the probable character components. Then, the stroke width of every component

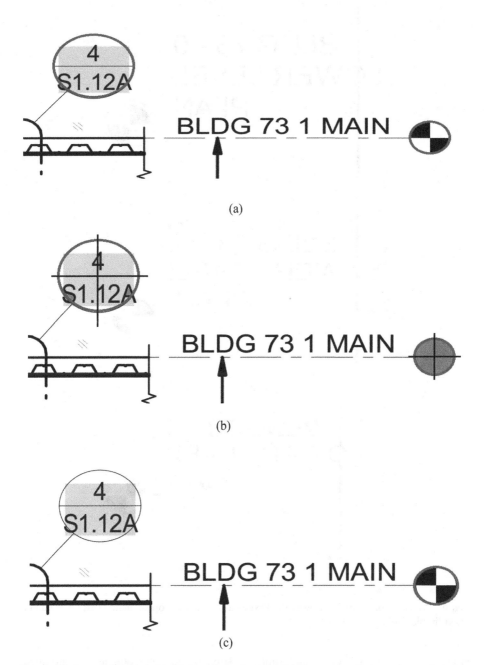

Fig. 5. (a) Detected circle is highlighted by red colour, (b) Contour analysis on detected circle, (c) Detected Elevation Datum is highlighted by red colour (Color figure online).

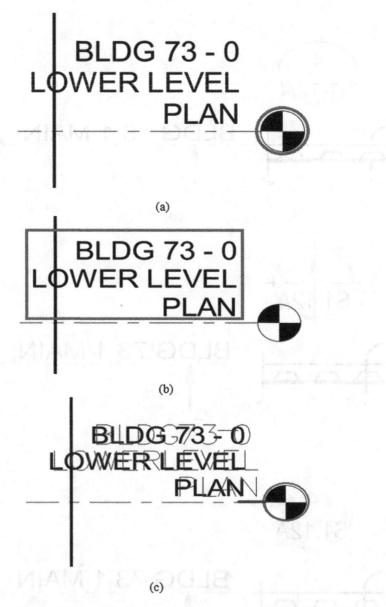

Fig. 6. (a) Elevation datum detection, (b) Text localization, (c) Corresponding text OCR output drawn in blue colour (Color figure online).

is compared with each other and similarly stroked-width components are grouped together. Since the text may extend to multiple lines, the component localization and grouping procedure is applied recursively. The diameter of the ED boundary is used as a distance measure to terminate the search mechanism. The aforesaid method is applied to both half of the image.

Fig. 7. Sectional line representation of Elevation Datum.

2.4 Optical Character Recognition of Localized Text

After the identification of the text components, we need to recognize these characters in order to proceed to hyperlink creation step. This is a very important step for hyperlink creation.

Now, for optical character recognition (OCR) there is Tesseract [11] open source engine, but the accuracy of tesseract engine falls if text is in italic or bold style. In most cases we need to extract information from small text region when tesseract fails to recognize properly. So, to sort out the problem of tesseract we have built an in-house OCR engine using a support vector machine classifier. An important step for accurate classification is the selection of proper features. The features can be of two types– local and global. Local features involve windowing the image whereas global feature takes some characteristics of the whole image. For local feature the image of the character is divided into 5×5 blocks. The features include the directional components of the border pixels in 4 directions. Thus, $5 \times 5 \times 4 = 100$ features are obtained. Some global features like aspect ratio, longest vertical run, normalized height of the leftmost, rightmost, and lowermost black pixel, Euler number etc. are also used to improve the accuracy. Thus, a total of 108 features are used for classification in the OCR system developed at ARC Document Solutions in collaboration with Indian Statistical Institute (ISI) [7]. The process of ED detection, text localization and corresponding text OCR outputs are shown in Fig. 6. A comparative study of tesseract and our In-build OCR result is shown in Table 3.

Table 2. Intermediate and final results at different stages

Process	Accuracy
Circle detection	98.02%
ED detection	97.56%
Text localization and recognition	98.75%
Hyperlinking with the documents	96.71%

3   Hyperlink Creation

After generating the OCRed text output, based on the experimental analysis, we used a post-processing module to validate the document naming convention. Finally, the

Now, we simply burn this information into the original document and end-up with clickable links which enable navigation among several plan documents within a particular project. Figure 8 represents navigation process from sheet source document to destination document **BLDG 73 – 0 LOWER LEVEL PLAN**.

4   Experimental Results

This section elaborates results including accuracy of our system based on the test on a dataset containing AEC drawing documents.

- **Data Collection**

ARC Document Solution provides a cloud system named as SKYSITE [12] which provides the architects to manage their documents. From the system we have collected AEC class of data from different architect. Nearly all the AEC drawing documents of a project, contain ED representations and the documents are navigated by creating hyperlinks to this notation. We have collected around 1140 different drawing documents. We have also added some data image where ED is not present. This was done to test the generic nature and robustness of our algorithm.

Table 3. Comparison study of OCR engine

Process	Tesseract	ARC OCR
Recognition	98.28%	98.75%
Average speed (ms)	200	148

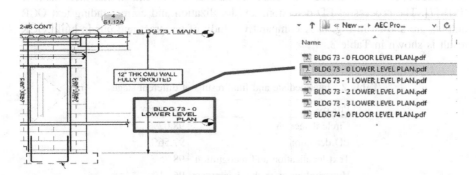

Fig. 8. Hyperlink navigation representation; When clicked on the Elevation Datum shape of a document, it will automatically navigate to the associated document i.e. BLDG 73 – 0 LOWER LEVEL PLAN.

- **Results and Accuracy**

In the first step we have detected circles from the document images. The accuracy of circle detection came out to be around 98.02% as shown in Table 2. Our goal is to detect Elevation Datum. After removal of false ED notations, the accuracy of detecting proper elevation datum is 97.56%. The next step is localization of destination sheet name text region and recognition of localized text. The OCR accuracy from the system developed to recognize 52 characters, 10 digits and a few symbols including dot (.) and dash (-), came out to be around 98.75%. The end to end automatic hyperlinking system accuracy is nearly 96.71%.

5   Conclusion and Future Work

We know that linking with the document and detection of the ED is of much necessity for any architect.

A good accuracy is needed for localization and linking. Though we obtained an accuracy of 96.71%, the system performance should further be improved. The cases where the documents are noisy or multiple straight lines either pass through or overlap the datum, the proposed method results in misclassification of the datum. Therefore, we guesstimate that the removal of such lines from the datum images followed by an image in-painting mechanism applied on these filtered datums can resolve the aforesaid problems. Also, there are some exceptional cases where our method doesn't produce adequate results (Fig. 9). Still, a system with current level of accuracy should prove useful for the architects and engineers.

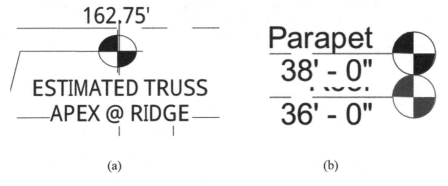

(a)   (b)

Fig. 9. (a) Destination sheet name appearing at Top and/or bottom of the elevation datum, (b) Overlapped elevation data.

References

1. Banerjee, P., Choudhary, S., Das, S., Majumder, H., Chaudhuri, B.B.: Automatic hyperlinking of engineering drawing documents. In: Document Analysis System (DAS), Santorini, Greece, pp. 103–107 (2016)
2. Najman, L., Gibot, O., Barbey, M.: Indexing technical drawings using title block structure recognition. In: Document Analysis and Recognition (DAS), vol. A247, pp. 587–591 (2001)
3. Illingworth, J., Kittler, J.: The adaptive hough transform. IEEE Trans. Pattern Anal. Mach. Intell. (PAMI) **5**, 690–698 (1987)
4. Cao, Y., Li, H.: Using engineering drawing interpretation for automatic detection of version information in CADD engineering drawing. Autom. Constr. **3**, 361–367 (2005)
5. Lu, Z.: Detection of text regions from digital engineering drawings. IEEE Trans. Pattern Anal. Mach. Intell. (PAMI) **4**, 431–439 (1998)
6. Banerjee, P., et al.: A system for creating automatic navigation among architectural and construction documents. In: Proceedings of the 14th IAPR International Conference on Document Analysis and Recognition (ICDAR) Kyoto, Japan (2017)
7. Banerjee, P., Chaudhuri, B.B.: An approach for bangla and devanagari video text recognition. In: Proceedings of International Workshop on Multilingual OCR (MOCR), Washington DC, USA (2013). article no. 8
8. Qureshi, R.J., Ramel, J.-Y., Barret, D., Cardot, H.: Spotting symbols in line drawing images using graph representations. In: Liu, W., Lladós, J., Ogier, J.-M. (eds.) GREC 2007. LNCS, vol. 5046, pp. 91–103. Springer, Heidelberg (2008). https://doi.org/10.1007/978-3-540-88188-9_10
9. Pham, T., Delalandre, M., Barrat, S., Ramel, J.: Robust symbol localization based on junction features and efficient geometry consistency checking. In: Proceedings of the 12th International Conference on Document Analysis and Recognition, ICDAR 2013, pp. 1083–1087 (2013)
10. Do, T., Tabbone, S., Terrades., O.R.: Spotting symbol using sparsity over learned dictionary of local descriptors. In: Proceedings of the 11th IAPR International Workshop on Document Analysis Systems ICDAR 2014, pp. 156–160 (2014)
11. https://opensource.google.com/projects/tesseract
12. https://app.skysite.com/

Search and Classification

Multimodal Classification of Document Embedded Images

Matheus Viana[1]([✉]), Quoc-Bao Nguyen[2], John Smith[2], and Maria Gabrani[3]

[1] IBM Research Brazil, Rua Tutóia, 1157, São Paulo 04007-900, Brazil
mviana@br.ibm.com
[2] IBM Thomas J. Watson Research Center, 1101 Kitchawan Road, Route 134,
Yorktown Heights, NY 10598, USA
[3] IBM Zurich Research Laboratory, Smerstrasse 4, 8803 Rschlikon, Switzerland

Abstract. Images embedded in documents carry extremely rich information that is vital in its content extraction and knowledge construction. Interpreting the information in diagrams, scanned tables and other types of images, enriches the underlying concepts, but requires a classifier that can recognize the huge variability of potential embedded image types and enable their relationship reconstruction. Here we tested different deep learning-based approaches for image classification on a dataset of 32K images extracted from documents and divided in 62 categories for which we obtain accuracy of $\sim 85\%$. We also investigate to what extent textual information improves classification performance when combined with visual features. The textual features were obtained either from text embedded in the images or image captions. Our findings suggest that textual information carry relevant information with respect to the image category and that multimodal classification provides up to 7% better accuracy than single data type classification.

1 Introduction

Images embedded in scientific, or other professional documents, such as financial reports, clinical trials report or internal company corpora, carry important visual information densely packed and structured. These images can represent many categories, such as diagrams, scanned tables, lesions in medical photos, scatter plots, and so on. Understanding the content of these images is crucial to answer questions that may not be possible by simply analyzing what is written in the document. For instance, one may want to know the average profit per year of a company based on a financial report that contains a table of profit per month. In another scenario, one may want to know whether there is a positive trend in a scatter plot. Obtaining the correct answer for these questions is a rather complex task in case the answer is not explicitly written in the main text. The first step towards a solution is to recognize the type of image one is dealing with. Next, the image is analyzed and its content is extracted in a category-dependent fashion. This process allows the construction of a knowledge graph for understanding concepts present in images and their relationships.

© Springer Nature Switzerland AG 2018
A. Fornés and B. Lamiroy (Eds.): GREC 2017, LNCS 11009, pp. 45–53, 2018.
https://doi.org/10.1007/978-3-030-02284-6_4

An important point is that, in most common applications, the image recognition is performed by an image classifier that relies on visual features to decide what is the most appropriated category. For instance, this is the case for most studies in document categorization and retrieval [6,9], functional decomposition [1] and modality detection of biomedical images [13].

However, many types of images also have relevant information in form of written text in addition to visual features. For instance, the word ocean may indicate that the image is a map, as well as the word chart may indicate a pie chart. This textual information can be extracted through OCR engines. A similar approach was used in [8,11,15], where the authors applied OCR to document images to extract textual features and to perform different tasks, such as document categorization and functional decomposition.

A less explored type of information corresponds to the captions of document images. In [2] the authors used images caption to perform the classification of images in three different classes. In this paper, we report the results of different experiments related to image classification. First, we tested different state-of-the-art network architectures to perform deep learning-based image classification. We also show that fusion techniques can improve the classification accuracy. Finally, we show that textual information extracted either from images via OCR engines or image captions carry important information and add significant level of accuracy per se.

To address the vast representation variability and extract the underlying structure we propose a multimodal deep learning approach which has been tested on two datasets described in Sect. 2. We present results in Sect. 3 and conclude the paper with discussion and summary in Sect. 4. In addition to testing different architectures for image classification.

The main contributions of our paper are *(i)* the systematic investigation of different networks architectures for classification of document images in a large number of classes; *(ii)* combination of both visual and textual features for classification of document images, where the textual features are obtained from OCR engines or images caption.

2   Methods and Datasets

2.1   Large Dataset

We generated a dataset of 32K images obtained from different sources, such as scientific papers, financial reports, medical reports and web search engines. The images were manually classified into 62 different categories that cover different domains such as *general, geological* and *molecular*. A few examples of images are shown in Fig. 1a. The goal was to use this dataset to investigate the performance of different deep learning-based methods in the task of document images classification.

The dataset was split into training (40%), validation (30%) and test (30%) for purposes of training convolutional neuronal networks (CNNs). We tested three CNN architectures, ResNet [7], Inception V3 [14] and Xception [3]. We also performed fusion experiments by extracting features from the last layer of the CNNs and using them as input of SVM classifiers. We divide the fusion experiments into *average*, *stack* and *concat*, depending on how the features from two CNNs are combined.

We also used this dataset to test whether textual features extracted via OCR from the images could improve the performance of our classifiers. To do so, each image from our dataset was submitted to the Tesseract OCR engine to have their embedded text extracted. The resulting text of all the images were combined to generate a bag of words. We used the function spellcheck from the python library *textblob* to remove noisy words. We also used a snowball stemmer algorithm to reduce similar words to a common radical. Upon having this bag of words, each image was represented as binary vector where the i-th position is one if the i-th word of our bag does appear in the image. Finally, the binary vectors were used as input for a SVM classifier.

2.2 Small Dataset

We also generated a dataset of images extracted from papers from ArXiv. We downloaded all the 1425 documents that contained the word *seismic* in the abstract (as on Mar 15, 2018). We used PDFFigures [4] to extract metadata from these documents. PDFFigures is a tool that identifies tables and figures together with their corresponding captions. In total we extracted 3501 images and captions which have been manually classified into 6 classes, such as *plot*, *heat map* and *diagram*. Out of the total images extracted, we excluded 5.4% corresponding to text regions incorrectly extracted as images. Notice that this number is in agreement with the accuracy reported in [4]. Another 1.4% incorporated some part of the main text and had to have their bounding box manually adjusted. We did not use the tables extracted with PDFFigures and our goal was to use this small dataset to evaluate how the textual features extracted from the captions could improve the performance of our document images classifiers.

The PDF documents were converted into plain text files by using the *pdftotext* tool from the Poppler library (https://poppler.freedesktop.org/). All the text files have been pre-processed with same noise-removal and stemmer algorithms mentioned in the previous section and concatenated to create a representative corpora of our documents. The corpora contains $\sim 800K$ words and was used to train a *word2vec* algorithm with dimension 64 [12]. The trained *word2vec* model has a vocabulary of $\sim 30K$ words and was used to make inference over every image caption creating a numeric embedding representation of size 64 for each of these captions.

As mentioned above, the ground-truths classes of both large and small datasets were assigned by hand through visual inspection of each image.

3 Results

We used the large dataset described in Sect. 2.1 to test different deep learning-based approaches for classifying images extracted from documents. The results are summarized in Table 1. We found that the fusion technique of extracting features from CNNs and using them as input of SVM classifier improves the baseline classification performance. Because transfer learning has been proven to be a successful approach for classifying document's images, [6], with exception of the networks marked with "*" in Table 1, all networks have been pre-trained on the ImageNet dataset. Only the last layer of those networks was fine-tuned on our dataset. The ResNet architectures marked with "*" have been trained from scratch and their number of layers was selected by optimizing the model accuracy in the range 50 to 101 layers.

Table 1. Classification performance of different architectures of neuronal networks on our testing set. Baseline represents the performance of a given network alone, while FE+SVM represented the performance obtained combining feature extraction from CNN and SVM classifier. Only best results are shown.

Model	Experiment	Input size	Acc. (%)
ReNet*101	baseline	256×256	76.79
ResNet*50	baseline	512×512	81.85
ReNet*101	FE+SVM	256×256	83.43
ReNet*50	FE+SVM	512×512	83.07
ReNet*58	baseline	128×128	84.63
ReNet*58	FE+SVM	128×128	84.98
ReNet*82	baseline	128×128	84.53
ReNet*82	FE+SVM	128×128	84.42
ReNet*(101+50)	FE+SVM (stack)	256×256 512×512	83.26
ReNet*(101+50)	FE+SVM (average)	256×256 512×512	84.88
ReNet*(101+50)	FE+SVM (concat)	256×256 512×512	84.41
InceptionV3	baseline	128×128	62.3
InceptionV3	baseline	256×256	78.87
Xception	baseline	256×256	75.21
Xception	baseline	512×512	81.03

Results in Table 1 indicates that the best performance in classifying images extracted from documents is achieved with input size 128×128. This is somehow intriguing given that larger images are capable of retaining fine grain image details. The best performance was achieved by using RestNet with 58 layers for extracting the features that feed to a SVM classifier. Also interesting that adding more layers (from 58 to 82) does not improve accuracy, which highlights the importance of selecting the appropriate number of layers.

We also used our large dataset to test whether the text embedded in the images together with the images themselves are capable of improving the classification accuracy. We found however that this type of data is very sparse as shown in Fig. 1b. In fact, less than 5% of our images displayed at least one word captured by the OCR engine.

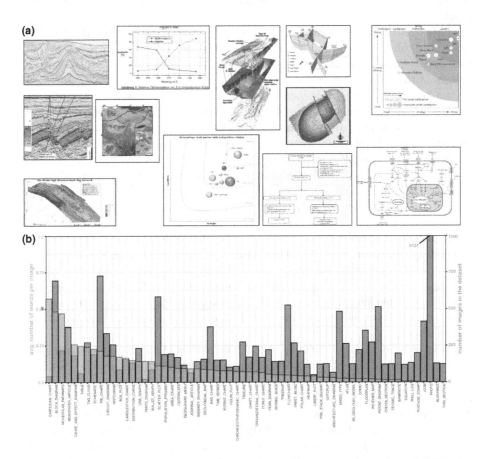

Fig. 1. (a) A few examples of images in our large dataset of 32K images. (b) Distribution of number of image in each class of our large dataset and average number of words fond by the OCR engine in each image for each class. The sparsity of the textual information in our dataset prevents us from using this type of data in a more effective way to improve image classification.

Despite the sparsity of this data, as a proof of concept that textual features embedded in images extracted from documents has some potential to positive affect the image classification performance, we created a subdataset in which we keep only the categories *block diagram* and *pie charts* for which we found a reasonable words to image ratio (∼0.37 words per image and 20% of the images display at least one word). By using a four-layers multilayer perceptron (MLP; 256, 128, 64 and 2 units), we observed that textual features in isolation are capable of classifying the subdataset images with accuracy 8% above the baseline expected by chance. By inspecting the weights of the first layer of the MLP, we found the most relevant words are *start, input, program, director, information* and *diagram*, which seems to be words that often appear in images of class *block diagram*.

This result indicates that this data modality carries important information that could contribute to improve image classification. To test this hypothesis, we used the Xception network with input size of 128×128 to extract features from images of the subdataset and we combined these features with those generated by the 3rd layer of the MLP mentioned above. The concatenated features were used as input for a three-layers MLP (2048, 1024 and 2 units) responsible for classifying the images as *block diagram* or *pie chart*. We found that the combination of textual and visual features increases by 1% the accuracy in the testing set (acc. 0.92% vs 0.93%, respectively).

The previous result indicates that textual features carry additional information capable of improving classification accuracy when combined with visual features. To further explore the potential of multimodal classification, we used our small dataset described in Sect. 2.2 that combines visual features and textual features extracted from image captions. The textual features are encoded in a embedding representation created by using *word2vec* model. To check whether this type of representation carry any relevant information about the image category, we used *t-Stochastic Neighbor Embedding* (tSNE) [10] to reduce the embedding dimensionality from 64 to 2 as shown in Fig. 2a. The figure reveals some spatial structure, suggesting that image captions can be used for image classification.

Next, we tested the performance of a classifier based on textual features only. We used a four-layers MLP (256, 128, 64 and 6 units) to classify the captions embedding into one of the six classes. We split the data into training and testing sets (90% and 10%, respectively) and trained the model for 512 epochs. The maximum model accuracy on the testing set observed after 1024 epochs of training was 70.8%, which is significantly higher than what is expected by chance ($\sim$17%, see Fig. 2b). Although the experiments have been conducted in different datasets, this result suggests that figure captions have a lot more potential for classification of document figures than text embedded in the figures.

To check whether figure captions could contribute to improve image classification, we used the Xception network with input size of 128×128 to perform visual features extraction and we combined these features with the captions embedding. The concatenated features were used as input for a three-layers MLP (2048, 1024 and 2 units). As shown in Fig. 2c, we found the maximum accuracy in the testing set was about 7% greater than what is obtained when using visual features alone (79.6%).

To gain some insights of how the textual features combined with visual features are boosting the classification accuracy of document images, we inspected

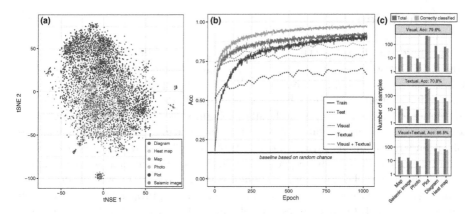

Fig. 2. (a) Embedding of document figure captions. A *word2vec* model of size 64 was trained on the corpora of all arXiv papers with the word *seismic* in the abstract. The embedding was created by applying word-by-word the trained model to every caption extracted out of those documents. We used *t-Stochastic Neighbor Embedding* (tSNE) [10] to reduce the embedding dimensionality from 64 to 2. (b) Accuracy for train and testing set as we train our single and multimodal models. (c) Classification performance of our best trained models for each class.

one sample (shown in Fig. 3 that was miss-classified by the Xception network that only uses visual features only. Without textual features, the image shown was classified as a *map*. Combining visual and textual features from its caption, the image was correctly classified as *diagram*. In Fig. 3 we also show the most relevant words of the corresponding caption that help in the correct image classification. We notice that words related to the concept of graph, such as *network, vertices, edge* and *connected*, display high importance for the correct classification, which is reasonable taking into account that the category *diagram* contains many examples of graphs and flowcharts.

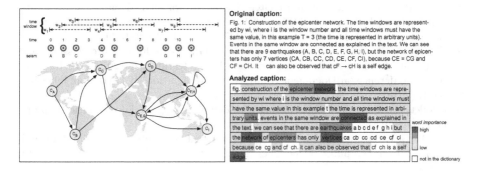

Fig. 3. Figure extracted from [5] that was correctly classified as *diagram* when using visual and textual features together. We also show the impact each word had for the image classification.

4   Conclusion

Image understanding is a crucial part in the process of document-based knowledge construction. As part of this step, image classification is of fundamental importance so that appropriate algorithms can be applied to specific types of images for content extraction. Here we used a large dataset to show how feature extraction combined with SVM classifier can improve the process of image classification. We also investigate the role of textual features in boosting image classification when combined with visual features. First we show how text extracted from images through OCR engines can be used as an additional source of information for image classification. Although some improvement was observed, we found this feature to be very spare and its use require appropriate high-resolution datasets for which OCR engines are reliable and for which the text extraction make sense. Finally, we used a small dataset that contains images extracted from documents and their captions to further explore the combination of visual and textual features. A corpora was created and used to train a word2vec model. The model was used for creating an embedding representation for each caption. By means of tSNE 2D projection we observed that the embedding displays spatial structure in terms of images categories. We found a significant performance improvement ($\sim$7%) in image classification when visual features extracted via ConvNet were combined with textual features represented by captions embedding. Our results also suggest that the use of textual information is more effective for particular classes of images, such as *diagrams* and less effective for other classes, such as *photo* (see Fig. 2). In future experiments we would like to test different approached for weighted multimodal classification, i.e. classification of images based on different types of data such data each data has a different weight depending on the image class. These weights will be embedded in the deep learning algorithm such that the whole system can be trained in a end-to-end fashion.

References

1. Chao, H., Fan, J.: Layout and content extraction for PDF documents. In: Marinai, S., Dengel, A.R. (eds.) DAS 2004. LNCS, vol. 3163, pp. 213–224. Springer, Heidelberg (2004). https://doi.org/10.1007/978-3-540-28640-0_20
2. Cheng, B., Stanley, R.J., Antani, S., Thoma, G.R.: Graphical figure classification using data fusion for integrating text and image features. In: 2013 12th International Conference on Document Analysis and Recognition (ICDAR), pp. 693–697. IEEE (2013)
3. Chollet, F.: Xception: Deep learning with depthwise separable convolutions. arXiv preprint (2016)
4. Clark, C.A., Divvala, S.K.: Looking beyond text: extracting figures, tables and captions from computer science papers. In: AAAI Workshop: Scholarly Big Data (2015)
5. Ferreira, D.S., Ribeiro, J., Papa, A.R., Menezes, R.: Towards evidences of long-range correlations in seismic activity. arXiv preprint arXiv:1405.0307 (2014)

6. Harley, A.W., Ufkes, A., Derpanis, K.G.: Evaluation of deep convolutional nets for document image classification and retrieval. In: 2015 13th International Conference on Document Analysis and Recognition (ICDAR), pp. 991–995. IEEE (2015)
7. He, K., Zhang, X., Ren, S., Sun, J.: Deep residual learning for image recognition. In: Proceedings of the IEEE Conference on Computer Vision and Pattern Recognition, pp. 770–778 (2016)
8. Ittner, D.J., Lewis, D.D., Ahn, D.D.: Text categorization of low quality images. In: Symposium on Document Analysis and Information Retrieval, pp. 301–315. Citeseer (1995)
9. Kang, L., Kumar, J., Ye, P., Li, Y., Doermann, D.: Convolutional neural networks for document image classification. In: 2014 22nd International Conference on Pattern Recognition (ICPR), pp. 3168–3172. IEEE (2014)
10. Maaten, L.V.D., Hinton, G.: Visualizing data using T-SNE. J. Mach. Learn. Res. **9**, 2579–2605 (2008)
11. Maderlechner, G., Suda, P., Brückner, T.: Classification of documents by form and content. Pattern Recognit. Lett. **18**(11–13), 1225–1231 (1997)
12. Mikolov, T., Sutskever, I., Chen, K., Corrado, G.S., Dean, J.: Distributed representations of words and phrases and their compositionality. In: Advances in Neural Information Processing Systems, pp. 3111–3119 (2013)
13. Miranda, E., Aryuni, M., Irwansyah, E.: A survey of medical image classification techniques. In: International Conference on Information Management and Technology (ICIMTech), pp. 56–61. IEEE (2016)
14. Szegedy, C., Vanhoucke, V., Ioffe, S., Shlens, J., Wojna, Z.: Rethinking the inception architecture for computer vision. In: Proceedings of the IEEE Conference on Computer Vision and Pattern Recognition, pp. 2818–2826 (2016)
15. Taylor, S.L., Lipshutz, M., Nilson, R.W.: Classification and functional decomposition of business documents. In: Proceedings of the Third International Conference on Document Analysis and Recognition, vol. 2, pp. 563–566. IEEE (1995)

Searching for a Compressed Polyline with a Minimum Number of Vertices (Discrete Solution)

Alexander Gribov[✉]

Esri, 380 New York Street, Redlands, CA 92373, USA
agribov@esri.com

Abstract. There are many practical applications that require the simplification of polylines. Some of the goals are to reduce the amount of information, improve processing time, or simplify editing. Simplification is usually done by removing some of the vertices, making the resultant polyline go through a subset of the source polyline vertices. If the resultant polyline is required to pass through original vertices, it often results in extra segments, and all segments are likely to be shifted due to fixed endpoints. Therefore, such an approach does not necessarily produce a new polyline with the minimum number of vertices. Using an algorithm that finds the compressed polyline with the minimum number of vertices reduces the amount of memory required and the postprocessing time. However, even more important, when the resultant polylines are edited by an operator, the polylines with the minimum number of vertices decrease the operator time, which reduces the cost of processing the data. A viable solution to finding a polyline within a specified tolerance with the minimum number of vertices is described in this paper.

Keywords: Polyline compression · Polyline approximation
Orthogonality · Circular arcs

1 Introduction

The task is to find a polyline within a specified tolerance of the source polyline with the minimum number of vertices. That polyline is called optimal. Usually, a subset of vertices of the source polyline is used to construct an optimal polyline [6,8]. However, an optimal polyline does not necessarily have vertices coincident with the source polyline vertices. One approach to allow the resultant polyline to have flexibility in the locations of vertices is to find the intersections between adjacent straight lines [11] or geometrical primitives [4]. However, there are situations when such an approach does not work well, for example, when adjacent straight lines are almost parallel to each other or a circular arc is close to being tangent to a straight segment.

Another task is to find a polyline within the specified tolerance of the source polyline with the minimum number of vertices while maintaining orthogonal

© Springer Nature Switzerland AG 2018
A. Fornés and B. Lamiroy (Eds.): GREC 2017, LNCS 11009, pp. 54–68, 2018.
https://doi.org/10.1007/978-3-030-02284-6_5

angles. In this case, the orthogonal polyline cannot be restricted by the vertices of the source polyline. Similar to the previous task, the vertices of the resultant polyline can be found as the intersections between adjacent straight lines [12]. This solution works well; however, it does not have a proper error model for the joints.

The approach described in this paper evaluates a set of vertex locations (considered locations) while searching for a polyline with the minimum number of vertices. This approach leads to a robust algorithm for compression of polylines.

2 Compression of a Polyline with a Minimum Number of Vertices

The algorithm to find the compressed polyline with a minimum number of vertices is based on three concepts:

- The vertices of the resultant polyline can only be from the set of considered locations.
- Verification that the resultant segment or geometrical primitive can properly describe the corresponding part of the source polyline: points of the source polyline do not deviate more than the tolerance from the segment, and changes of direction can be explained by the noise.
- The optimal solution is found by the dynamic programming approach.

2.1 Discretization of the Solution

Any compressed polyline must be within tolerance of the source polyline; therefore, the compressed polyline must have vertices within tolerance of the source polyline. It would be very difficult to consider all possible polylines and find one with the minimum number of vertices; therefore, as an approximation, only some discrete locations around the vertices of the source polyline are considered (see the black points around the vertices of the source polyline in Fig. 1).

The chosen locations around the vertices of the source polyline are on an infinite equilateral triangular grid with the distance from the vertices of the source polyline less than the specified tolerance. The equilateral triangular grid (see Fig. 2) has the lowest number of nodes compared to other grids (square, hexagonal, etc.), satisfying that the distance from any point to the closest node does not exceed the specified threshold.

Fig. 1. Example of one segment (red segment) between considered locations (black dots) within tolerance of the source polyline (blue polyline). (Color figure online)

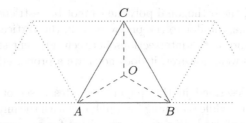

Fig. 2. The worst case distance for the equilateral triangular grid is the distance from the center of the triangle O to any vertex of the equilateral triangle. If $OA = OB = OC = q$, then $AB = BC = CA = \sqrt{3}q$.

The chosen length of the side of an equilateral triangle in the equilateral triangular grid is calculated from the error it introduces. That error can be expressed as a proportion of the specified tolerance. For example, $q \in (0, 1)$ proportion of the specified tolerance means that the side of the equilateral triangle is equal to $\sqrt{3}q$ times the specified tolerance. This leads to about $\dfrac{2\pi}{3\sqrt{3}q^2} \approx \dfrac{1.2}{q^2}$ locations for each vertex. To decrease complexity, some locations might be skipped if they are considered neighbor vertices of the source polyline; however, it should be done without breaking the dynamic programming approach described in Sect. 2.5. If tolerance is great, it is possible to consider locations around segments of the source polyline. In this paper, to support any tolerance, only locations around the vertices of the source polyline are considered. Densification of the source polyline might be necessary to find the polyline with the minimum number of vertices.

2.2 Testing a Segment to Satisfy Tolerance

For a compressed polyline to be within tolerance, every segment of the compressed polyline must be within tolerance of the part of the source polyline it describes. To find the compressed polyline with the minimum number of vertices, this test has to be performed many times (testing different segments between considered locations). Precalculated convex hulls can be used to perform such tests efficiently [14], [10, Appendix II]. The complexity of this task is $O(\log^2(n))$, where n is the number of vertices in the convex hull.[1]

If there are no lines with a thickness of two tolerances covering the convex hull completely, then one segment cannot describe this part of the source polyline. The complexity of this check is $O(n)$.

---

[1] The expected number of points in the convex hull for the N random points in any rectangle is $O(\log(N))$, see [13]. If the source polyline has parts close to an arc, the size of the convex hull tends to increase. In a worst case, the number of vertices in the convex hull is equal to the number of vertices in the original set.

2.3   Testing Segment Endpoints

The test described in Sect. 2.2 does not check the ends of the segment. The example in Fig. 3 shows that the source polyline changes directions several times (zigzag) before going up. Without checking endpoints and changes in direction, the compressed polyline might not describe some parts of the source polyline (Fig. 3a). Therefore, these tests are necessary to guarantee that the compressed polyline (Fig. 3b) describes the source polyline without missing any parts.

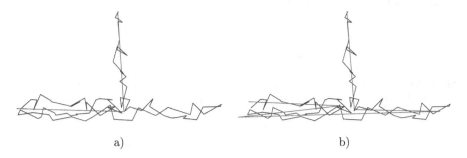

a)   b)

Fig. 3. The blue polyline is the source polyline. The red polyline is the result of the algorithm without checking for endpoints and the source polyline direction (a) and with both checks performed (b). (Color figure online)

The test to determine whether segment endpoints are within the tolerance of the part of the source polyline is based on the convex hull in the same way as the test performed in Sect. 2.2.

The same test for tolerance can be used if the segment extends in parallel and perpendicular directions (see Fig. 4) and contains a convex hull as part of the source polyline it describes. If more directions are used, a better approximation of the curved polygon can be obtained. The complexity of the test is $O\big(\log^2(n)\big)$, see [10, Appendix II].

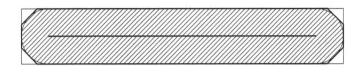

Fig. 4. The diagonal striped area is the tolerance area around the segment. The thin rectangle is the approximation of the area around the segment. A thick polygon would be a better approximation.

2.4   Testing Polyline Direction

The test for the source polyline to have a zigzag is performed by checking if the projection to the segment of backward movement exceeds two tolerances ($2T$, where T is the tolerance). Two tolerances are used because one vertex of the source polyline can shift forward by the tolerance and another vertex can shift backward by the tolerance, see Fig. 5. The algorithm is based on analyzing zigzags before the processed point. Let p_i, $i = \overline{0..N - 1}$, be the vertices of the polyline and N be the number of vertices in the polyline. The next algorithm constructs a table for efficient testing.

Fig. 5. Example of two points following each other on the source polyline, when one vertex is shifting forward and another vertex is shifting backward by the tolerance T.

Define a set of directions $\alpha_j = \dfrac{2\pi}{N_d} j$, where $j = \overline{0..N_d - 1}$, N_d is the number of directions.

Cycle over each direction α_j, $j = \overline{0..N_d - 1}$.

    Define the priority queue with requests containing two numbers. The first number is the real value, and the second number is the index. The priority of the request is the first number.

    Set $k = 0$.

    Cycle over each point p_i of the source polyline, $i = \overline{0..N - 1}$.

        Calculate the projection of p_i to the direction α_j (scalar product between the point and the direction vector):

$$d = p_i \cdot \left(\cos\left(\alpha_j\right), \sin\left(\alpha_j\right) \right).$$

        Remove all requests from the priority queue with a priority of more than $d + 2T$. If the largest index from removed requests is larger than k, set k equal to that index.

        Set $V_{j,i} = k$.

        Add request $(d, i + 1)$ to the priority queue.

To test if the part of the source polyline between vertices i_s and i_e has a zigzag:

First, find the closest direction α_j to the direction of the segment α_{j*}:

$$j^* = \text{round}\left(\frac{N_d}{2\pi} \alpha \right) \bmod N_d, \text{ where } \alpha \text{ is the direction of the segment.}$$

Second, if $V_{j^*, i_e} \leq i_s$, then there are no zigzags for the segment describing the part of the source polyline from vertex i_s till i_e.

Let $W_i = \min_{0 \leq j \land j < N_d}(V_{j,i})$. If $i_s < W_{i_e}$, then one segment cannot describe the part of the source polyline from vertex i_s till i_e.

This test has the following limitations:

- Since the tested direction is only an approximation of the closest one, the result is also an approximation.
- For some error models, a zigzag might pass the test. For example, if errors are limited by a circle, a zigzag by two tolerances is only possible if it happens directly on the segment.

Nevertheless, it is an efficient test to avoid absurd results, like in Fig. 3a. The complexity of the algorithm is $O(N_d N \log(N))$, and the complexity to test any segment is $O(1)$.

2.5 Dynamic Programming Approach to Find an Optimal Solution

The optimal solution is found by using the dynamic programming approach, see [11,18,20].

Let $p_{i,j}$ be considered locations for vertex p_i, where $i = \overline{0..N-1}$, $j = \overline{0..N_i-1}$, N_i is the number of considered locations for the vertex i. Let pairs (i_k, j_k), $k = \overline{0..m}$, divide the source polyline into m straight segments $(p_{i_k,j_k}, p_{i_{k+1},j_{k+1}})$ describing the source polyline from vertex i_k to i_{k+1}, $k = \overline{0..m-1}$. Note that neighbor segments are already connected in p_{i_k,j_k}, $k = \overline{1..m-1}$, and this solution avoids problems in algorithms [4,11] when the intersection of neighbor segments is far away from the source polyline.

The goal of this algorithm is to find a polyline with the minimum number of vertices while satisfying tolerance restriction, and among all polylines find one with the minimum integral of squared deviations. Therefore, minimization is performed in two parts $\left\{\begin{array}{c} T^{\#} \\ T^{\epsilon} \end{array}\right\}$, where the first part $T^{\#}$ is the number of segments, and the second part T^{ϵ} is the integral of the squared deviations between segments and the source polyline. The solutions are compared by the number of segments and, if they have the same number of segments, by the integral of squared deviations between segments and the source polyline. The solution of this task, when the optimal polyline has vertices coincident with the source polyline, can be found in [5].

Let P_k, $k = \overline{0..N-1}$ be parts of the source polyline from vertex 0 to k.

The optimal solution is found by induction. Define the optimal solution for polyline P_0 as $\left\{\begin{array}{c} T^{\#}_{0,j} \\ T^{\epsilon}_{0,j} \end{array}\right\} = \left\{\begin{array}{c} 0 \\ 0 \end{array}\right\}$, $j = \overline{0, N_0 - 1}$. For $k = \overline{1, N-1}$, construct the optimal solution for P_k from optimal solutions for $P_{k'}$, $k' = \overline{0..k-1}$.

$$\left\{\begin{array}{c} T^{\#}_{k,j} \\ T^{\epsilon}_{k,j} \end{array}\right\} = \min_{\substack{0 \leq k' \land k' < k \\ 0 \leq j' \land j' < N_{k'} \\ \text{check}\,((k',j'),(k,j))}} \left(\left\{\begin{array}{c} T^{\#}_{k',j'} + 1 \\ T^{\epsilon}_{k',j'} + \epsilon_{(k',j'),(k,j)} \end{array}\right\} \right), \quad (1)$$

where $\epsilon_{(k',j'),(k,j)}$ is the integral of squared deviations between a segment $(p_{k',j'}, p_{k,j})$ and the source polyline from vertex k' to k, check $((k',j'),(k,j))$ is a combination of checks described in Sects. 2.2, 2.3, and 2.4 to check if segment $(p_{k',j'}, p_{k,j})$ can represent the part of the source polyline from vertex k' to k.

The complexity of the algorithm can be reduced by the approach described in [11, Sect. 4]. The lower limits for the (1) when $k' \in [k_1, k_2]$ are derived in Appendix. The maximum of (5) and (6) can be used to skip checking combinations between vertices k_1 and k_2.

To reconstruct the optimal solution, it is necessary for $\begin{Bmatrix} T_{k,j}^{\#} \\ T_{k,j}^{\epsilon} \end{Bmatrix}$ to store $\{k', j'\}$ when the right part of (1) is minimal. The optimal solution is reconstructed from $\min\limits_{0 \le j \wedge j < N_{N-1}} \begin{Bmatrix} T_{N-1,j}^{\#} \\ T_{N-1,j}^{\epsilon} \end{Bmatrix}$ by recurrently using stored $\{k', j'\}$ values.

2.6 Compression of Closed Polylines

To find the optimal compression of a closed polyline, it is necessary to know the starting vertex. It is also necessary that the resultant polyline starts and ends in the same considered location. The next algorithm will be used to find the starting vertex and to construct a closed resultant polyline.

1. Construct a convex hull for all vertices of the source polyline.
2. Find the smallest angle of the convex hull polygon.
3. Take the vertex corresponding to the smallest angle as the starting vertex and reorient the closed polyline to start from that vertex.
4. Apply the algorithm.
5. From the constructed solution, take one vertex in the middle as the new starting vertex and reorient the closed polyline to start from that vertex.
6. Apply the algorithm once more. For the first and the last vertices consider only the location of the previous solution for the middle vertex.

Steps 1, 2, and 3 are important for small closed polylines, because the resultant polyline is likely to be within the tolerance of the source polyline, even with suboptimal orientation. As a consequence, without these steps, step 5 may not find the optimal division of the source polyline, leading to a suboptimal solution.

This algorithm does not guarantee finding the optimal solution, but it is a good compromise between the optimality of the resultant closed polyline and the speed.

2.7 Optimal Compression by Straight Segments and Arcs

The algorithm described in this paper is extendible to support arcs. The arc passing through considered locations differs from the segment because of the need to define the radius. Unfortunately, this adds significant complexity to the algorithm. Nevertheless, such an algorithm is possible. There are different ways to fit an arc into a polyline: minimum integral of squared differences of squares [15,19]; minimum integral of squared deviations [3,7,9,16,17]; minimum deviation; etc. The most efficient algorithms to fit an arc have constant complexity [7,9,15,19]; however, algorithms based on integral of squared differences of squares [15,19] might break for small arcs and, therefore, are not suitable. Checking that the part of the source polyline is within tolerance, endpoints, and zigzags will be time-consuming due to complexity $O(n)$.

2.8   Analysis of the Algorithm Complexity

The algorithm contains three steps:

1. Preprocessing of the source polyline: Construction of convex hulls (Sect. 2.2) and filling arrays for an efficient zigzag test (Sect. 2.4).
2. Construction of the optimal solution (Sect. 2.5).
3. Reconstruction of the optimal solution (Sect. 2.5).

A significant amount of time is spent on constructing an optimal solution. It is difficult to evaluate the complexity described in Appendix; however, the worst complexity is

$$O\left(N^2 \cdot \left(\max_{0 \le i \wedge i < N} N_i\right)^2 \cdot \log^2(N)\right). \tag{2}$$

The complexity of the algorithm depends on the type of polyline it processes; therefore, it is difficult to conclude what is the practical complexity of this algorithm. If the optimal polyline does not have segments describing too many vertices of the source polyline, (2) tends to be

$$O\left(N \cdot \left(\max_{0 \le i \wedge i < N} N_i\right)^2\right). \tag{3}$$

Figure 6 shows how much time it takes to process a polyline depending on the number of vertices. The dependence is very close to linear, supporting (3).

Figure 7 shows the dependence on the error introduced by a discrete set of considered locations (see Sect. 2.1) to the efficiency of the compression. Flexibility in places where neighboring segments connect to each other is very important to reach maximum compression, especially for noisy data.

2.9   Example

If the source polyline is the noisy version of a ground truth polyline, where the noise does not exceed some threshold, and the algorithm is provided with a tolerance slightly greater than the threshold to account for approximations inside the algorithm, then the resultant polyline will never have more vertices than the ground truth polyline. The effectiveness of this approach is shown in Fig. 8. Nine segments are sufficient to represent the arc with specified precision. The algorithm not only optimizes the number of segments, it also finds the locations of the segments that minimize integral of squared deviations.

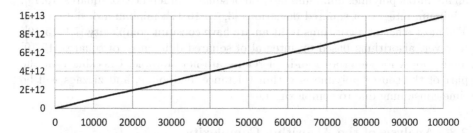

Fig. 6. Time needed to process a polyline versus the number of vertices. The time is measured in CPU ticks on the processor Intel Xeon CPU E5-2670. The polylines are generated using the Brownian motion process. Each next vertex is incremented from the previous vertex by random vector, with components normally distributed with zero mean and 0.25 standard deviation. The tolerance was set to one. The average reduction in the number of vertices is about 50 times.

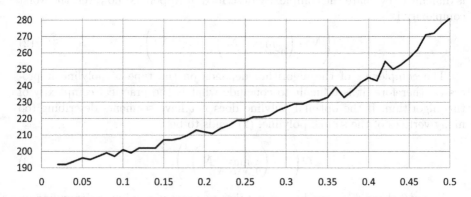

Fig. 7. The number of segments versus discretization error. The polyline was generated using the Brownian motion process in the same way as in Fig. 6 with 10,000 vertices.

Fig. 8. The black polyline is the source polyline. The red circles are the vertices of the optimal polyline. Ground truth is the arc of 90°. The noise has uniform distribution in the circle of one percent of the arc radius. (Color figure online)

3   Compression of a Polyline with a Minimum Number of Vertices by Orthogonal Directions

Reconstruction of orthogonal buildings requires support by 90° and sometimes 45°. Therefore, the square grid for considered locations is more appropriate for this task compared to the triangular grid that supports directions by 60°. Because only certain directions are allowed, only segments between pairs of considered locations aligned by these directions may be parts of the resultant polyline. Suppose the resultant segment goes between vertex i and j, it has to be within tolerance of all vertices between i and j; therefore, it goes through their considered locations (with the exception of the segment deviating close to the tolerance due to discretization of considered locations).

The optimal solution is found by induction. Define the optimal solution for polyline P_0 as $\begin{Bmatrix} T^{\#}_{0,j,q} \\ T^{\epsilon}_{0,j,q} \end{Bmatrix} = \begin{Bmatrix} 0 \\ 0 \end{Bmatrix}$, where $j = \overline{0, N_0 - 1}$, $q = \overline{0, M - 1}$, and M is the number of different directions. For orthogonal case $M = 4$, and for 45° case $M = 8$. Take directions as $\alpha_i = \dfrac{360°}{M} \cdot i$, $i = \overline{0, M - 1}$. For $k = \overline{1, N - 1}$, construct the optimal solution for P_k from the optimal solution for P_{k-1}.

$$\begin{Bmatrix} T^{\#}_{k,j,q} \\ T^{\epsilon}_{k,j,q} \end{Bmatrix} = \min_{\substack{0 \le j' \wedge j' < N_{k-1} \\ 0 \le q' \wedge q' < M \\ 2|q' - q| \ne M \\ \text{angle}\,(p_{k,j} - p_{k-1,j'}, \alpha_{q'})}} \left(\begin{Bmatrix} T^{\#}_{k-1,j',q'} + \delta_{q' \ne q} \\ T^{\epsilon}_{k-1,j',q'} + \epsilon_{(k-1,j'),(k,j)} \end{Bmatrix} \right),$$

where angle (v, α) is the check that the vector v has angle α (zero length vectors are allowed) and $\delta_{q' \ne q} = \begin{cases} 1, & \text{if } q' \ne q; \\ 0, & \text{otherwise.} \end{cases}$

The condition $2|q' - q| \ne M$ corresponds to prohibiting changes in direction by 180°.

For the 45° case, it is possible to restrict the resultant polyline from having sharp angles by not allowing a change of direction by 135°
$(|4 - ((q' - q) \bmod 8)| \ne 1)$.

Note that it is not necessary to check for the tolerance, direction, and end-points because they are satisfied during each induction step.

Analyzing the previous solution along M direction will further reduce the amount of calculations. The total complexity of the algorithm is

$$O\left(N \cdot \max_{0 \le i \wedge i < N} (N_i) \cdot M \right).$$

For some data, the algorithm may produce an improper result. This happens when the introduction of a zero length segment lowers the penalty.

Because the correct orientation is not known in advance, it is necessary to rotate polylines by different angles and take the solution with the lowest penalty [12, see Sect. 6].

The main difference between the algorithm described in this section and [12] is in the parameters. The algorithm described in this paper uses tolerance, while the algorithm in [12] is based on the penalty Δ for each additional segment. Specification of the tolerance guarantees that the resultant polyline is within the tolerance of the source polyline.

3.1 Examples

Figure 9a shows an example of the reconstruction of orthogonal buildings. The reconstruction of buildings with 45° sides are shown in Fig. 9b.

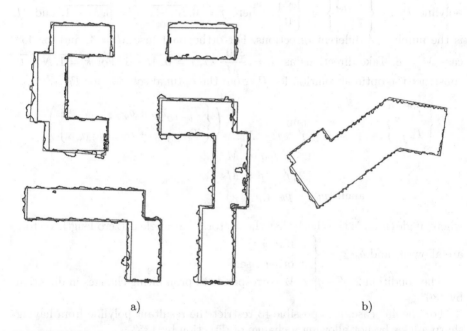

a)   b)

Fig. 9. The black polylines are reconstructed buildings from lidar data [1]. The red polylines are the resultant orthogonal shapes (a), and resultant shape with orthogonal and diagonal sides (b). The blue polylines are the ground truth taken from [2]. (Color figure online)

The performance was analyzed on a dataset with 4, 681 buildings on two Intel Xeon CPU E5-2670 processors with 32 threads (see Fig. 10). Reconstruction of orthogonal shapes from polylines took 30 s, and orthogonal and diagonal sides took 1 min 30 s.

Fig. 10. The red polylines are the resultant orthogonal shapes. The result is overlapped with imagery to evaluate quality of the method. (Color figure online)

4   Conclusion

This paper describes an algorithm that finds a polyline approximately with the minimum number of vertices while satisfying tolerance restriction. The solution is optimal with the following limitations:

- The vertices of the compressed polyline are limited to considered locations (Sect. 2.1).
- The test that the vertex of the compressed polyline is located between some vertices of the source polyline is approximate due to the snapping of the breaking point (Appendix).
- The tests for endpoints (Sect. 2.3) and zigzags are approximate (Sect. 2.4).

The performance of the algorithm can be greatly improved if the number of considered locations is decreased without losing quality. This requires further research.

Modification of this algorithm to find a compressed polyline when angles between adjacent segments are restricted to 90° or 45° has the following important differences:

- The algorithm requires densification of the source polyline.
- The complexity of the algorithm becomes proportional to the number of points in the densified source polyline.

- The complexity of the algorithm becomes inversely proportional to the square of the precision parameter q, which was defined in Sect. 2.1.

The advantages of this algorithm are as follows:

- While this task can be solved by using the dynamic programming approach without considered locations, the advantage of this approach is in satisfying the tolerance requirement in the joints of the resultant orthogonal polyline. Different types of tolerance restrictions at the joints can be supported by adjusting the set of considered locations.
- The algorithm has complexity proportional to the length of the source polyline.
- This algorithm requires that the tolerance be specified, which is easier than specifying the penalty Δ in [12].

The limitation of this algorithm is its inability to work with small tolerances because the complexity of the algorithm is inversely proportional to the tolerance. This limitation is not an issue for processing real data because they always come from measurements and there are no measuring devices that can measure without some error.

Acknowledgments. The author would like to thank Linda Thomas and Mary Anne Chan for proofreading this paper; and Arthur Crawford for helpful discussions and processing the data from [1,2] used in Figs. 9 and 10. The author would also like to thank the anonymous reviewers for their helpful comments to improve this paper.

Appendix: Lower Bounds for an Optimal Solution

Following the approach described in [11, Sect. 4]

$$
\begin{aligned}
&\min_{\substack{k_1 \le k' \wedge k' \le k_2 \\ 0 \le j' \wedge j' < N_{k'} \\ \text{check}\,((k',j'),(k,j))}} \left(\left\{ \begin{array}{l} T^{\#}_{k',j'} + 1 \\ T^{\epsilon}_{k',j'} + \epsilon_{(k',j'),(k,j)} \end{array} \right\} \right) \gtrsim \\
&\gtrsim \min_{\substack{k_1 \le k' \wedge k' \le k_2 \\ 0 \le j' \wedge j' < N_{k'}}} \left(\left\{ \begin{array}{l} T^{\#}_{k',j'} + 1 \\ T^{\epsilon}_{k',j'} + \epsilon^{(k_2)}_{(k',j'),(k,j)} \end{array} \right\} \right),
\end{aligned}
\tag{4}
$$

$$
\text{where } \epsilon^{(k_2)}_{(k',j'),(k,j)} = \min_{\substack{0 \le j_2 \wedge j_2 < N_{k_2} \\ \text{check}\,((k',j'),(k_2,j_2)) \\ \text{check}\,((k_2,j_2),(k,j))}} \left(\epsilon_{(k',j'),(k_2,j_2)} + \epsilon_{(k_2,j_2),(k,j)} \right).
$$

From (4), it follows that

$$\min_{\substack{k_1 \leq k' \wedge k' \leq k_2 \\ 0 \leq j' \wedge j' < N_{k'} \\ \text{check}\,((k',j'),(k,j))}} \left(\left\{ \begin{array}{l} T^{\#}_{k',j'} + 1 \\ T^{\epsilon}_{k',j'} + \epsilon_{(k',j'),(k,j)} \end{array} \right\} \right) \gtrapprox$$

$$\gtrapprox \min_{\substack{0 \leq j_2 \wedge j_2 < N_{k_2} \\ \text{check}\,((k_2,j_2),(k,j))}} \left(\left\{ \begin{array}{l} T^{\#}_{k_2,j_2} \\ T^{\epsilon}_{k_2,j_2} + \epsilon_{(k_2,j_2),(k,j)} \end{array} \right\} \right) \tag{5}$$

and

$$\gtrapprox \min_{0 \leq j_1 \wedge j_1 < N_{k_1}} \left(\left\{ \begin{array}{l} T^{\#}_{k_1,j_1} \\ T^{\epsilon}_{k_1,j_1} \end{array} \right\} \right) + \left\{ \begin{array}{c} 1 \\ \min_{\substack{0 \leq j_2 \wedge j_2 < N_{k_2} \\ \text{check}\,((k_2,j_2),(k,j))}} \left(\epsilon_{(k_2,j_2),(k,j)} \right) \end{array} \right\}. \tag{6}$$

The inequalities (5) and (6) are approximate due to the use of considered locations. However, this allows finding stricter limitations for the solution inside the interval and simultaneously finding the solution for breaking at vertex k_2.

It is possible to construct (5) and (6) with exact inequalities by constructing the optimal solution when the endpoint is not required to end in the considered location. Similarly, the part from vertex k_2 to (k,j) should not be required to end in the considered locations for vertex k_2.

References

1. Missouri spatial data information service. http://msdis.missouri.edu/data/lidar/index.html
2. Saint Louis County, Missouri. http://www.stlouisco.com/OnlineServices/MappingandData
3. Bodansky, E., Gribov, A.: Approximation of polylines with circular arcs. In: Lladós, J., Kwon, Y.-B. (eds.) GREC 2003. LNCS, vol. 3088, pp. 193–198. Springer, Heidelberg (2004). https://doi.org/10.1007/978-3-540-25977-0_18
4. Bodansky, E., Gribov, A.: Approximation of a polyline with a sequence of geometric primitives. In: Campilho, A., Kamel, M. (eds.) ICIAR 2006. LNCS, vol. 4142, pp. 468–478. Springer, Heidelberg (2006). https://doi.org/10.1007/11867661_42
5. Chan, W.S., Chin, F.: Approximation of polygonal curves with minimum number of line segments or minimum error. Int. J. Comput. Geomet. Appl. 06(01), 59–77 (1996). https://doi.org/10.1142/S0218195996000058
6. Chen, F., Ren, H.: Comparison of vector data compression algorithms in mobile GIS. In: 2010 3rd IEEE International Conference on Computer Science and Information Technology (ICCSIT), vol. 1, pp. 613–617, July 2010. https://doi.org/10.1109/ICCSIT.2010.5564118

7. Dorst, L.: Total least squares fitting of k-Spheres in n-D Euclidean space using an (n+2)-D isometric representation. J. Math. Imaging Vis. **50**(3), 214–234 (2014). https://doi.org/10.1007/s10851-014-0495-2

8. Douglas, D.H., Peucker, T.K.: Algorithms for the reduction of the number of points required to represent a digitized line or its caricature. Cartographica Int. J. Geograph. Inf. Geovisualization **10**(2), 112–122 (1973). https://doi.org/10.3138/fm57-6770-u75u-7727

9. Gribov, A.: Approximate fitting of circular arcs when two points are known. ArXiv e-prints, May 2015. http://arxiv.org/abs/1504.06582

10. Gribov, A.: Optimal compression of a polyline with segments and arcs. ArXiv e-prints, April 2016. http://arxiv.org/abs/1604.07476

11. Gribov, A., Bodansky, E.: A new method of polyline approximation. In: Fred, A., Caelli, T.M., Duin, R.P.W., Campilho, A.C., de Ridder, D. (eds.) SSPR/SPR 2004. LNCS, vol. 3138, pp. 504–511. Springer, Heidelberg (2004). https://doi.org/10.1007/978-3-540-27868-9_54

12. Gribov, A., Bodansky, E.: Reconstruction of orthogonal polygonal lines. In: Bunke, H., Spitz, A.L. (eds.) DAS 2006. LNCS, vol. 3872, pp. 462–473. Springer, Heidelberg (2006). https://doi.org/10.1007/11669487_41

13. Har-Peled, S.: On the expected complexity of random convex hulls. CoRR abs/1111.5340, December 2011. http://arxiv.org/abs/1111.5340

14. Hershberger, J., Snoeyink, J.: Speeding up the Douglas-Peucker line-simplification algorithm. In: Proceedings of the 5th International Symposium on Spatial Data Handling, pp. 134–143 (1992)

15. Ichoku, C., Deffontaines, B., Chorowicz, J.: Segmentation of digital plane curves: a dynamic focusing approach. Patt. Recogn. Lett. **17**(7), 741–750 (1996). https://doi.org/10.1016/0167-8655(96)00015-3

16. Landau, U.M.: Estimation of a circular arc center and its radius. Comput. Vis. Graph. Image Process. **38**(3), 317–326 (1987). https://doi.org/10.1016/0734-189X(87)90116-2

17. Robinson, S.M.: Fitting spheres by the method of least squares. Commun. ACM **4**(11), 491 (1961). https://doi.org/10.1145/366813.366824

18. Safonova, A., Rossignac, J.: Compressed piecewise-circular approximations of 3D curves. Comput.-Aided Des. **35**, 533–547 (2003). https://doi.org/10.1016/S0010-4485(02)00073-8

19. Thomas, S.M., Chan, Y.T.: A simple approach for the estimation of circular arc center and its radius. Comput. Vis. Graph. Image Process. **45**(3), 362–370 (1989). https://doi.org/10.1016/0734-189X(89)90088-1

20. Yin, L., Yajie, Y., Wenyin, L.: Online segmentation of freehand stroke by dynamic programming. In: Eighth International Conference on Document Analysis and Recognition, vol. 1, pp. 197–201, August 2005. https://doi.org/10.1109/ICDAR.2005.180

Optical Music Recognition

Pen-Based Music Document Transcription with Convolutional Neural Networks

Javier Sober-Mira[1], Jorge Calvo-Zaragoza[2]([✉]), David Rizo[1],
and José M. Iñesta[1]

[1] Department of Software and Computing Systems, University of Alicante,
Alicante, Spain
{jsober,drizo,inesta}@dlsi.ua.es
[2] Schulich School of Music, McGill University, Montréal, Canada
jorge.calvozaragoza@mcgill.ca

Abstract. The transcription of music sources requires new ways of interacting with musical documents. Assuming that automatic technologies will never guarantee a perfect transcription, our intention is to develop an interactive system in which user and software collaborate to complete the task. Since the use of traditional software for score edition might be tedious, our work studies the interaction by means of electronic pen (e-pen). In our framework, users trace symbols using an e-pen over a digital surface, which provides both the underlying image (offline data) and the drawing made (online data). Using both sources, the system is capable of reaching an error below 4% when recognizing the symbols with a Convolutional Neural Network.

Keywords: Music documents · Optical music recognition
Pen-based technologies · Convolutional Neural Networks

1 Introduction

Automatic recognition systems have been traditionally focused on accomplishing a fully-automated operation, yet optimum performance cannot be assured [2,8, 18]. The management of the errors produced by the system is usually seen as an issue outside the research process because it is simply considered as the procedure for converting the system hypothesis into the desired result. Quite often, however, we find a semi-automatic scenario in which the human operator has the eventual responsibility of verifying and completing the task [15].

This approach to problem solving by using pattern recognition algorithms with the user in the loop, has been successfully used in different tasks, like image retrieval [10], speech transcription, and machine translation [16], among others. In a domain closer to that presented in this paper, user feedback has been successfully used in word spotting in historical printed documents [11].

© Springer Nature Switzerland AG 2018
A. Fornés and B. Lamiroy (Eds.): GREC 2017, LNCS 11009, pp. 71–80, 2018.
https://doi.org/10.1007/978-3-030-02284-6_6

All these works have in common the demonstration of a clear benefit when taking advantage of the intervention of the human expert in the process.

In this paper, we focus on the human-machine interaction for tasks related to music notation. The automatic transcription of music documents into a symbolic format is a complex task [14], and their current performance do not allow us to consider them reliably in a fully-automatic scenario [4]. Therefore, it seems interesting to set out the aforementioned interactive paradigm when dealing with the task of music document transcription. However, conventional channels of communication such as the keyboard or the mouse are not easily applicable. On the contrary, handwriting is a natural way of communication for humans, and so it is interesting to consider it for interacting with the computer. This can be done by means of electronic pen (e-pen) technologies [9].

When using this kind of interfaces, the user is provided with a friendlier interface to interact, but the result of the interaction is no longer deterministic: unlike the keyboard or mouse entry, for which it is clear what the user is inputting, the pen-based interaction has to be decoded and this process might have errors [6].

This work focuses on early music notation handwritten scores (see Fig. 1). The music sheets will be transcribed into the symbolic domain and stored in an XML format, suitable to be post-processed. We cannot assume an absolute accuracy in the system performance, so the output score post-editing might be tedious and time-consuming. The suitable understanding of this kind of documents are not within the reach of every expert, and those who can actually correct the system output still prefer to work with pencil and paper for these tasks, so they are more comfortable using pen-based technologies for human-computer interaction involving music documents [5]. This is why our objective is to provide an ergonomic interface with an e-pen able to provide low error recognition rates.

The use of the e-pen produces an interesting multimodal signal, which can be used to boost the recognition [1,17]. To carry out this classification task, we make use of Convolutional Neural Networks [19]. Within this paradigm, we can nicely combine the different modalities produced so that the performance can be improved as far as possible.

Fig. 1. The kind of documents processed are in Spanish white mensural notation that are transcribed into an XML representation.

Note that the approach proposed here does not attempt to ignore automatic recognition strategies. That is, we do not expect users to manually trace every single symbol of an image. Ideally, one would initially use an automatic system, and then use the interface proposed here to post-process the output in a more ergonomic way.

The rest of the paper is organized as follows. First, the kind of handwritten score data and how they are represented are introduced in Sect. 2. Then, the convolutional neural network architecture used will be described in Sect. 3, followed by the way in which the unimodal and multimodal decisions are made (Sect. 4). Finally, the results (Sect. 5) and conclusions (Sect. 6) are summarized.

2 Data and Multimodal Representation

We assume a workflow in which the user traces symbols on a digital surface depicting a music score. The system, therefore, receives a multimodal signal: on one hand, the sequence of points that indicates the path followed by the e-pen on the digital surface —usually referred to as *online* modality—; on the other hand, the piece of image below the drawn, which contains the original traced symbol —*offline* modality—. The goal is to use this interaction to transcribe the musical document. Since the interaction itself gives us the position of the symbols in the image, it is only necessary to infer which type of symbol has been traced in each interaction.

Figure 2 illustrates the process explained above for a single symbol. The actual information obtained is the sequence of 2D points in the same order they were collected, indicating the path followed by the e-pen (*online* information). An image representation of the symbol can be rendered by generating segments between pairs of consecutive points. In addition, we can consider the bounding box of the pen strokes to crop the original image, thereby obtaining the symbol of interest as it appears in the original image (*offline* information).

The process for collecting and labeling the dataset has been implemented on a graphical interface specifically designed for this work. See Fig. 3 for an illustration of the user interface.

To carry out our experiments, we consider a dataset consisting of 60 pages of handwritten documents in Spanish White Mensural notation (circa 16th and 17th centuries) including 10 150 symbols of 30 different classes (see Table 1)[1]. Each sample is represented by both the offline (region-of-interest image) and the online (image reconstructed from the user traces) modalities. Data were collected by five different users, tracing symbols on an archive of early music handwritten in Mensural notation. The number of symbols per class is not balanced but it depicts the same distribution found in the documents.

---

[1] The dataset is freely available at http://grfia.dlsi.ua.es/ (Bimodal music symbols from Early notation).

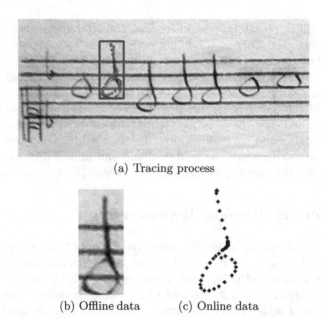

(a) Tracing process

(b) Offline data   (c) Online data

Fig. 2. Example of extraction of a *minima* note. Above, the sequence of points collected by the e-pen. The box represents the bounding box defined from the sequence of user traces. Below, the multimodal data extracted.

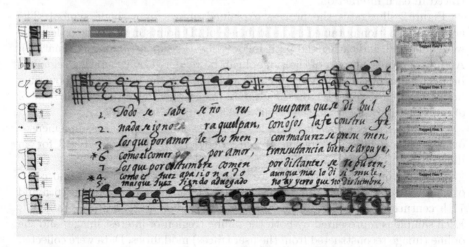

Fig. 3. Snapshot of the graphical interface developed and used for tagging. On the right, the images of the score pages are presented for selection. The central window is the main one, where the user can see the contents of the image and proceed to make the symbol tracing. On the left side, the result of the classification (trace, region of interest, and output class) can be seen.

Table 1. A representative subset of the elementary mensural symbols in the archive that have been used as classes for the classifier.

Group	Some classes of symbols			
Note	Semibrevis	Minima	Col. Minima	Semiminima
	o	♩	♪	♪
Rest	Longa	Brevis	Semibrevis	Semiminima
	│	ı	ı	r
Clef	C Clef	G Clef	F Clef (I)	F Clef (II)
	‖	♦	?	♯♦
Signature	Major	Minor	Common	Cut
	¢2	C3	C	¢
Others	Flat	Sharp	Dot	Custos
	♭	♯	.	～

3   Classification Scheme

The classification scheme utilized are different Convolutional Neural Networks (CNN), which have shown a great success in a number of tasks related to computer vision [12]. These networks take advantage of local filters, pooling, and many connected layers to learn a suitable data representation for classification tasks.

The architecture of our CNN is depicted in Fig. 4. The same scheme is utilized for classifying both the offline and online images. As mentioned above, the traces made by the user are converted into an image, in order to represent both modalities in the same way to be provided to the network. Input layers are of the same size for both cases (36×36), so traces and bounding box images are resized to these dimensions.

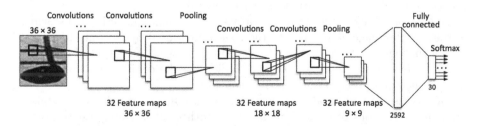

Fig. 4. CNN architecture utilized for both the offline and online inputs.

We denote by $Conv(c, k)$ a spatial convolutional layer with kernel size $k \times k$ and number of filters c, with Rectified Linear Unit (ReLU) activation [7]. Therefore, the CNN we have evaluated for our approach comprises the following configuration: $Conv(32, 3) \rightarrow Conv(32, 3) \rightarrow MaxPool(2) \rightarrow Conv(32, 3) \rightarrow Conv(32, 3) \rightarrow MaxPool(2)$.

After two series of convolutions and pooling layers, the neurons are arranged into a hidden layer that is fully-connected to a SoftMax output with 30 units. This last layer permits us to interpret the activation of every unit as the probability of the input signal x to represent each considered class, ω: $P(\omega|x)$ [3].

4   Classification Strategies

Several strategies have been considered to address the classification of the multimodal data:

Single Modalities. It is interesting to measure how well each modality images considered are able to perform the classification of the music symbols. To this end, we consider the *single mode* classification strategies, which means to assess the performance of the CNN in Fig. 4 for the images of one modality by itself.

This analysis may be also useful to check whether the staff present as background in the offline mode image makes the problem harder or not, which would pose the need to apply staff removal algorithms.

Multimodal Classifications. The main goal of this paper is to check how the combination of different sources of information can be used to improve a hard classification task like the present one. Two kind of information fusions have been tested depending on where the different data were actually combined.

- **Intermediate fusion:** the two images are supplied to the input layer of two CNNs, but the two networks end up in a single output layer.
- **Late fusion:** the decisions of each single CNN are interpreted in terms of probabilities that are combined into a single decision.

For the intermediate fusion scheme, the neural codes computed from both images are concatenated into a single hidden layer of the network that is fully connected to the softmax output layer (see Fig. 5).

In this case, the classification is performed by a maximum activation scheme, so the sample image is assigned to the class represented by the output neuron having the highest activation. Due to the SoftMax layer, the output of the CNN corresponds to values between 0 and 1, indicating the confidence (probability) that the network gives to each possible category.

In the case of multimodal classification by late fusion, the decision is taken from the activations of the output layer for both single-architecture networks. Since they can be interpreted as the probabilities assigned by each network to the

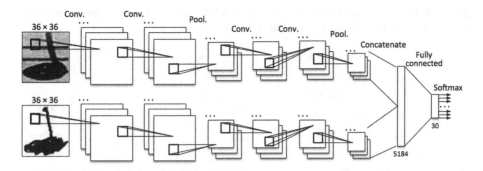

Fig. 5. CNN architecture utilized for the intermediate fusion approach.

offline and online representations of the sample, the decisions of the independent CNNs can be merged by a linear combination.

Let Ω denote the set of categories considered. Given images x and y from the offline and online modality, respectively, the late fusion emits the label $\hat{\omega}$ such that

$$\hat{\omega} = \arg\max_{\omega \in \Omega} \frac{1}{2} P_{\text{offline}}(\omega|x) + \frac{1}{2} P_{\text{online}}(\omega|y),$$

where $P_{\text{offline}}(\omega|x)$ and $P_{\text{online}}(\omega|y)$ are the probabilities obtained from the corresponding modality.

5   Results

Experimentation followed a 5-fold cross-validation scheme for the four classification approaches considered. The independent folds were randomly created with the sole constraint of having the same number of samples per class (when possible) in each of them.

Error rates achieved by the different classification schemes are presented in Table 2. Average and standard deviations for the five folds are displayed.

Regarding the single-modality classifications, it is interesting to note that the offline mode performs better, although not dramatically (1%), than the online one. Although this may seem contradictory according to the literature [13], it is important to emphasize that the writers of each modality are not the same. Thus, we can deduce that the original copyists were more cautious when writing, and therefore their handwriting is easier to classify. On the other hand, current users pay less attention to the way they write, which makes online mode more complex to decode in our experiments.

Another conclusion that can be made from these results is that, the presence of the staff lines in the offline region of interest, has not made the classification task harder, since in the online mode the staff is not present and this was not an advantage for it.

What is very significant is the difference between the results obtained by the single modalities and the multimodal approaches. The experiments report that

Table 2. Results (error rates) obtained for a 5-fold cross validation experiment with respect to the four classification schemes considered.

Classification strategy	Average ± std. dev.
Offline modality	6.3 ± 0.7
Online modality	7.3 ± 0.2
Late fusion	3.6 ± 0.5
Intermediate fusion	3.5 ± 0.7

both multimodal classification schemes significantly outperformed the strategies only using one modality. In this case, less than 4% of the symbols are mislabeled, achieving figures that are around half of the former.

The differences were no significant when comparing the performance of both multimodal approaches. The computation time is neither significantly greater in one case or in the other.

6   Conclusions

This paper presents a new approach to transcribe music documents by means of a computer equipped with e-pen technologies. Our framework produces a multimodal signal by which music symbol classification can be improved.

This framework also provides a more comfortable and user-friendly environment for expert musicologists to interact with the system.

Experimentation with a particular corpus of handwritten Spanish white mensural notation has been presented, considering CNNs as classification scheme. Results of classification of the single modalities considered and two different multimodal fusion strategies have been presented.

Results support that it is worth to consider both modalities in the classification process, as accuracy is noticeably improved with a combination of them than that achieved by the single modalities. Very low rates (around 3.5%) were obtained when combining both modalities. This promising performance makes it possible an efficient work by the expert.

This is a first step to achieve a complete system for music document transcription. More factors are still of interest, such as detecting the position of the symbols in the staff or check the impact of different writers or experts in the interactions with the system.

As the classification learns from the data images, the approach is independent of the notation. The training phase adapts the system to it, so it can be applied to any kind of notation or style of writing. The actual impact of these variations is still needed to be studied.

Acknowledgment. This work was supported by the Social Sciences and Humanities Research Council of Canada, and by the Spanish Ministerio de Ciencia, Innovación y Universidades through Project HISPAMUS (No. TIN2017-86576-R supported by EU FEDER funds).

References

1. Azeem, S.A., Ahmed, H.: Combining online and offline systems for arabic handwriting recognition. In: Proceedings of the 21st International Conference on Pattern Recognition ICPR 2012, pp. 3725–3728 (2012)
2. Benetos, E., Dixon, S., Giannoulis, D., Kirchhoff, H., Klapuri, A.: Automatic music transcription: challenges and future directions. J. Intell. Inf. Syst. **41**(3), 407–434 (2013)
3. Bourlard, H., Wellekens, C.: Links between markov models and multilayer perceptrons. IEEE Trans. Pattern Anal. Mach. Intell. **12**(11), 1167–1178 (1990)
4. Donald Byrd and Jakob Grue Simonsen: Towards a standard testbed for optical music recognition: definitions, metrics, and page images. J. New Music Res. **44**(3), 169–195 (2015)
5. Calvo-Zaragoza, J., Oncina, J.: Recognition of pen-based music notation with finite-state machines. Expert Syst. Appl. **72**, 395–406 (2017)
6. Calvo-Zaragoza, J., Rizo, D., Quereda, J.M.I.: Two (note) heads are better than one: pen-based multimodal interaction with music scores. In: Proceedings of the 17th International Society for Music Information Retrieval Conference, ISMIR 2016, New York City, United States, pp. 509–514, 7–11 August 2016
7. Glorot, X., Bordes, A., Bengio, Y.: Deep sparse rectifier neural networks. In: Proceedings of the Fourteenth International Conference on Artificial Intelligence and Statistics, Fort Lauderdale, USA, pp. 315–323 (2011)
8. Graves, A., Mohamed, A.-R., Hinton, G.: Speech recognition with deep recurrent neural networks. In: 2013 IEEE International Conference on Acoustics, Speech and Signal Processing (ICASSP), pp. 6645–6649, May 2013
9. Keysers, D., Deselaers, T., Rowley, H.A., Wang, L.L., Carbune, V.: Multi-language online handwriting recognition. IEEE Trans. Pattern Anal. Mach. Intell. **39**(6), 1180–1194 (2017)
10. Kherfi, M.L.: Review of Human-Computer Interaction Issues in Image Retrieval, chapter 14, pp. 215–240 (2008)
11. Konidaris, T., Gatos, B., Ntzios, K., Pratikakis, I., Theodoridis, S., Perantonis, S.J.: Keyword-guided word spotting in historical printed documents using synthetic data and user feedback. Int. J. Doc. Anal. Recognit. (IJDAR) **9**(2), 167–177 (2007)
12. LeCun, Y., Bengio, Y., Hinton, G.: Deep learning. Nature **521**(7553), 436–44 (2015)
13. Plamondon, R., Srihari, S.N.: On-line and off-line handwriting recognition: a comprehensive survey. IEEE Trans. Pattern Anal. Mach. Intell. **22**(1), 63–84 (2000)
14. Rebelo, A., Fujinaga, I., Paszkiewicz, F., Marçal, A.R.S., Guedes, C., Cardoso, J.S.: Optical music recognition: state-of-the-art and open issues. Int. J. Multimedia Inf. Retrieval **1**(3), 173–190 (2012)
15. Toselli, A.H., Vidal, E., Casacuberta, F.: Multimodal Interactive Pattern Recognition and Applications, 1st edn. Springer, London (2011). https://doi.org/10.1007/978-0-85729-479-1
16. Vidal, E., Rodríguez, L., Casacuberta, F., García-Varea, I.: Interactive pattern recognition. In: Popescu-Belis, A., Renals, S., Bourlard, H. (eds.) MLMI 2007. LNCS, vol. 4892, pp. 60–71. Springer, Heidelberg (2008). https://doi.org/10.1007/978-3-540-78155-4_6
17. Vinciarelli, A., Perrone, M.P.: Combining online and offline handwriting recognition. In: Proceedings of 7th International Conference on Document Analysis and Recognition, pp. 844–848 (2003)

18. Yin, F., Wang, Q.-F., Zhang, X.-Y., Liu, C.-L.: ICDAR 2013 chinese handwriting recognition competition. In: 2013 12th International Conference on Document Analysis and Recognition (ICDAR), pp. 1464–1470, August 2013
19. Zeiler, M.D., Fergus, R.: Visualizing and understanding convolutional networks. In: Fleet, D., Pajdla, T., Schiele, B., Tuytelaars, T. (eds.) ECCV 2014. LNCS, vol. 8689, pp. 818–833. Springer, Cham (2014). https://doi.org/10.1007/978-3-319-10590-1_53

Optical Music Recognition by Long Short-Term Memory Networks

Arnau Baró[1]([✉]), Pau Riba[1], Jorge Calvo-Zaragoza[2], and Alicia Fornés[1]

[1] Computer Vision Center - Computer Science Department,
Universitat Autònoma de Barcelona, Bellaterra, Catalonia, Spain
{abaro,priba,afornes}@cvc.uab.cat
[2] Schulich School of Music, McGill University, Montreal, Canada
jorge.calvozaragoza@mcgill.ca

Abstract. Optical Music Recognition refers to the task of transcribing the image of a music score into a machine-readable format. Many music scores are written in a single staff, and therefore, they could be treated as a sequence. Therefore, this work explores the use of Long Short-Term Memory (LSTM) Recurrent Neural Networks for reading the music score sequentially, where the LSTM helps in keeping the context. For training, we have used a synthetic dataset of more than 40000 images, labeled at primitive level. The experimental results are promising, showing the benefits of our approach.

Keywords: Optical music recognition · Recurrent neural network
Long short-term memory

1 Introduction

Sheet music uses music notation to encode information on how to interpret a piece. It is one of the most considered means for the transmission of music. With the advent of the digital era, there is a number of computational tools for working with musical scores. However, to take advantage of these benefits, it is necessary to transcribe sheet music into a digital format that can be processed by a computer.

The transcription process can be carried out manually. However, the wealth of music notation inevitably leads to burdensome software for music score editing, which makes the whole process very time-consuming and prone to errors. Consequently, automatic transcription systems for musical documents represent interesting tools. The field devoted to address this task is known as Optical Music Recognition (OMR) [1–3]. Nowadays, there exist many commercial OMR tools, like PhotoScore[1] or SharpEye[2].

Typically, an OMR system takes an image of a music score and automatically exports its content into some structured format such as MEI or MusicXML. In

---

[1] http://www.neuratron.com/photoscore.htm.
[2] http://www.visiv.co.uk/.

© Springer Nature Switzerland AG 2018
A. Fornés and B. Lamiroy (Eds.): GREC 2017, LNCS 11009, pp. 81–95, 2018.
https://doi.org/10.1007/978-3-030-02284-6_7

addition to the automatic transcription of sheet music, the OMR field comprises many other applications such as writer identification, graphic reconstruction of old music scores, generation of audio files from images, or retrieval of the same piece from different authors.

The process of recognizing the content of a music score from its image is complex because it has to deal with many music-specific difficulties [2], such as the two-dimensional nature of the notation, the double component of music symbols,[3] the presence of the staff lines, and so on.

Traditionally, OMR has been approached considering multi-stage systems [1]. The different stages comprise several small sub-tasks such as image binarization [4], staff-line removal [5], or music symbol classification [6]. Our work, however, focuses on directly recognizing the music content appearing on an image.

We do assume that the image depicts a single staff section (e.g. scores for violin, flute, etc.), much in the same way as most text recognition research focuses on recognizing words appearing in a given line image [7]. Note that this is not a strong assumption, as there exist algorithms that achieve good performance for both isolating staff sections [8] and separating music and lyrics (accompanying text) [9]. For this reason, one can assume that staves are already segmented and, therefore, can be processed as a sequence.

To address this specific task, the proposed architecture is based on Recurrent Neural Networks (RNN), since they have been applied with great success to many sequential recognition tasks such as speech [10] or handwriting [7] recognition. Specifically, to avoid the vanishing gradient problem, Long Short-Term Memory (LSTM) units are considered. Moreover, Bidirectional LSTMs are used to benefit from context information.

As a scientific novelty, we address the OMR by separating the two components of the musical symbols: duration and pitch, both in terms of training and evaluation. This provides the RNN with greater robustness, as they can focus on the specific aspects that concern each component. Our experimental results demonstrate the viability of this approach, obtaining results that are close to optimal on an exhaustive set of musical staves.

The rest of the paper is organized as follows. Section 2 explores the state of the art. Section 3 describes the method, whereas Sect. 4 analyzes the results. Finally, conclusions and future work are drawn in Sect. 5

2   Related Work

This section overviews the key approaches in Optical Music Recognition, and also, overviews the Deep Learning architectures applied to music research that are relevant to the present work.

2.1   Optical Music Recognition

An OMR system aims to recognize each element located in the music score. Figure 1 illustrates the usual pipeline from a scanned music score to a machine-

---

[3] Symbols appear with specific duration (rhythm) and pitch (melody).

readable format. The steps are the following. First, the image is preprocessed to reduce problems in segmentation. Usually, before segmenting the musical symbols and/or primitives, the staff lines are removed. Hence, the segmentation task is simplified. Afterwards, the primitives are merged to form symbols. Some methodologies use rules or grammars in order to be able to validate and solve some ambiguities from the previous step. Finally, the musical description file (e.g. MusicXML, MEI) is created with the information of the previous steps. These steps are described in more detail next.

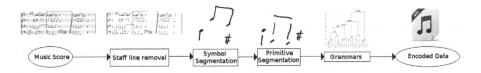

Fig. 1. Typical OMR pipeline.

The first stage is devoted to preprocessing and layout analysis. The most common techniques are binarization, noise removal and blur correction. However, other techniques as enhancement, skew correction or deskewing, among others have also been proposed. In music scores documents it is important to segment the document into regions. Authors in [11] propose a new algorithm to segment the regions that include text and regions containing music scores. Normally, the staff removal algorithm are based on projections and run-length analysis, contour-line tracking, or graphs.

The recognition of music symbols consists in the recognition of isolated and compound music symbols. Figure 2 shows examples of isolated and compound music symbols. This classification is done because the techniques are usually different. For example, isolated music symbols are usually detected by symbol recognition methods [12–15], grammar/rules [16], sequence analysis (e.g. Hidden Markov Models) [17,18], graphs [19], Multilayer perceptron [14] and deep neural networks [6,20,21]. In the case of compound music symbols, most methods are based on grammars or rules [22]. It must be noted that the combination of compound music symbols is large, so it is impossible to have examples of all these possible combinations. This limitation must be taken into account when developing learning-based approaches.

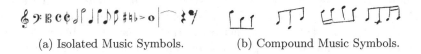

(a) Isolated Music Symbols.   (b) Compound Music Symbols.

Fig. 2. Examples of music symbols.

The validation stage is related to the previous one. Usually grammars or rules are defined to make more robust the recognition step in front of ambiguities.

Some works [16,22,23] propose the use of grammars to correct any mistakes as repeating or missing symbols. Another aspect that could be verified is whether the number of beats match the time signature.

OMR systems typically provide an output file at the end of the process. The most common output files are MIDI[4], MusicXML[5] or MEI[6]. MIDI (Musical Instrument Digital interface) is a communication technical standard used in electronic music devices. MusicXML is an open musical notation format based on Extensible Markup Language (XML). MEI is an open-source effort to define a system for encoding musical documents in a machine-readable structure.

2.2   Deep Learning in Music

According to Goodfellow, Bengio and Courvill [24], Deep Learning appeared between 1940s–1960s. However, it has become popular quite recently due to, among others, the technological advances in Hardware. In the last decade, several deep learning techniques have been applied to music or audio processing. For example, CNNs have been applied to audio processing in order to detect and recognize the sound of certain objects and scenes in videos. In [25] they use CNNs to compensate differences between video and audio sampling rates, whereas, the authors in [26] use CNN in order to process sounds. The authors of [27,28] have applied RNNs to MIDI generation, specifically LSTM in order to produce new music files taking advantage of sequence model of the music input files. In [29] RNNs are used in polyphonic music in order to make predictions.

As far as we know, there are very few deep learning-based systems that cover the whole stages of Optical Music Recognition. For example, a very recent OMR work which uses a Convolutional Sequence-to-Sequence network for recognizing printed scores has been published [30]. Then, Calvo-Zaragoza *et al.* [31] use an end-to-end architecture based on a Recurrent Convolutional Neural Network in order to recognize monophonic music scores. Finally, Pacha *et al.* [32] proposes a first step towards OMR developing a handwritten music symbol classifier. However, it is still far from a complete OMR system.

3   Methodology

Single staff sheet music can be seen as a sequence. In this way, a music score is read from left to right. In order to automatically process the music score and take into account the sequence of music symbols, a *Recurrent Neural Network* (RNN) seems an appropriate tool. In this work, we propose to make use of *Long Short-Term Memory* (LSTM) [33] networks. LSTMs have the ability to decide which information has to be kept as context and which information has to be removed, *i.e.* forgotten.

---

[4] https://www.midi.org/.
[5] http://www.musicxml.com/.
[6] http://music-encoding.org/.

Figure 3 shows the different stages of our proposed pipeline. Firstly, the input music scores are preprocessed (Subsect. 3.1). Afterwards, each column of the image is processed by an LSTM network (Subsect. 3.2). The output of the LSTM is passed by two fully connected layers in order to distinguish between rhythm and pitch (Subsect. 3.3). Finally, the output of the system is the recognition of symbols, including rhythm and pitch (Subsect. 3.4). The different steps of this pipeline are explained in the following sections.

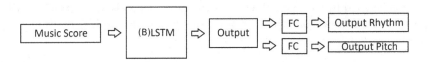

Fig. 3. Architecture of the network

3.1 Input

The proposed architecture is trained by batches of images that are resized to a fixed height of 50 pixels. Then, these images are fed into the proposed model using pixel-wise columns. The maximum width can be variable depending on the widest image in the batch. Therefore, images with a shorter width are padded with 0's to the maximum width of the batch. In this work, the staff lines have not been removed in order to avoid noise and distortions in the musical symbols. In addition, staff lines provide useful information in terms of the pitch. Note that features are not extracted from the image in order to maintain the spatial information and the spatial order as much as possible.

3.2 Long Short-Term Memory

A LSTM network has been used in order to recognize the elements of the sheet music. In this work, we use a bidirectional network to increase the performance and reduce ambiguities when recognizing some symbols. The combination of forward and backward pass allows to recognize symbols that may be confused if only one direction is used.

The proposed LSTM network is composed by 3 recurrent layers with a hidden state size of 128. We have trained our architecture for 100 epochs with a batch size of 128 or 64 for LSTM and BLSTM respectively. These values have been experimentally set. It must to be said that the network is trained column by column so it predicts one output per column. In other words, the output will end up being as long as the input image.

3.3 Fully Connected Layers

At the end of the LSTM network, we propose to use two heads in order to separately predict rhythm and melody. Therefore, after the LSTM output, two fully connected layers (FC) are used to obtain two different outputs. The reason to split the output in two parts is that the number of combinations between melody and rhythm is very high. In case of using a single output, all possible combinations of rhythm-melody must be created as possible classes. Therefore, we propose to exploit the idea that rhythm and pitch can be independent. Thus, rhythm is decided by the symbol whereas the pitch depends on the position with respect the staff lines. Following this idea, many more examples are available to train our system.

3.4 Output

After the FC layers, the next step is to calculate the loss and backpropagate the errors. Even though two heads are used to separate between rhythm and pitch, the output of our system should be able to deal with multiple classes per time step. Therefore, in validation and test, a threshold is applied to both outputs (Rhythm and Pitch) in order to obtain the corresponding classes. The outputs and the ground-truth of each music score is represented by two binary matrices, one for the rhythm and another for the melody or pitch. Horizontally, it corresponds to the width of the input image whereas the vertical axis tells the different classes for symbols and pitch, 54 and 26 respectively. Pitch corresponds to locations in the staff. Figure 4 shows the structure of the matrix for both melody Fig. 4a and rhythm Figs. 4b and 5 shows a real example with its corresponding groundtruth. The corresponding pixels where the symbol is located in the music score will be activated in both matrices indicating which symbols are activated in each time step *i.e.* pixels. The following symbols have been manually added to ease the recognition task:

- Epsilon (ε) is used to know where each symbol starts and ends, as it is used in text recognition. This symbol can be seen as a separator. Wherever this symbol is activated, it means that it is not possible to have any other symbol activated as well (see Fig. 4c blue marks). This symbol appears in both the rhythm and pitch ground-truths.
- *No note* is used to indicate that a symbol has not any pitch. This symbol only appears in the pitch ground-truth.

Finally, these outputs are converted into an array. One with the detection of the rhythm, another for the pitch and the last one with the combination of rhythm and pitch. These arrays will be used to evaluate the method.

3.5 Loss Function

In music, we can find one or more symbols in one instance of time, for example, chords or time signature (see Fig. 4c red marks). Therefore, a multilabel loss

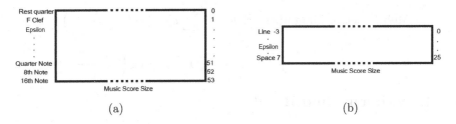

Fig. 4. Output representation for Rythm (a) and Pitch (b). (Color figure online)

Fig. 5. Example of Music Score and the corresponding Ground-truth in a Binary Matrix. The first row is the music score. The second row is the Rhythm Ground-truth. The third row is the Pitch Ground-truth.

function has to be chosen to deal with the before-mentioned problem. In other words, the loss function must allow more than one activation per time step. Thus, the softmax activation function cannot be used because it is thought for single-label classification problems. In this work, two different loss functions have been used: On the one hand, SmoothL1Loss creates a criterion that uses a squared term if the absolute element-wise error falls below 1 and an L1 term otherwise (Eq. 1). On the other hand, MultiLabelSoftMarginLoss creates a criterion that optimizes a multi-label one-versus-all loss based on max-entropy (Eq. 2). The loss is calculated independently for rhythm and melody. Once both losses are calculated, they are summed and backpropagated.

$$\text{SmoothL1Loss}(x, y) = \frac{1}{n} \sum \begin{cases} 0.5(x_i - y_i)^2, & \text{if } |x_i - y_i| < 1 \\ |x_i - y_i| - 0.5, & \text{otherwise} \end{cases} \quad (1)$$

$$\text{MultiLabelSoftMarginLoss}(x, y) = -\sum_i y[i] \cdot \log\left(\frac{1}{1 + e^{-x[i]}}\right)$$

$$+ (1 - y[i]) \log\left(\frac{e^{-x[i]}}{1 + e^{-x[i]}}\right) \quad (2)$$

4 Experiments and Results

This Section presents and discusses the experimental results.

4.1 Dataset

A Synthetic dataset has been used to train the network. This collection is composed of more than 50000 music scores with 3 different typographies. The dataset corresponds to incipts from the RISM catalog[7]. It is composed of almost 50000 music scores with 3 different typographies. The staffs are divided in 60% (29815) for training, 20% (9939) for validation and 20% (9939) for test.

4.2 Evaluation

The evaluation of a complete OMR system is not well defined in the literature. Thus, we propose to follow the evaluation described in [30]. The authors proposed to evaluate three aspects of the framework; pitch, rhythm and their combination. Note that the combination of pitch and rhythm corresponds to the performance of the whole system. The chosen evaluation metric is the *Symbol Error Rate* (SER) applied to an array produced by the system. Note that a threshold is applied to convert the output of the FC layers to an array of symbols.

Fig. 6. Example of music score.

An example of the format of the three output arrays, corresponding to Fig. 6, is the following.

- Rhythm: [gClef, accidental sharp, accidental sharp, accidental sharp, quarter note, eight note, bar line].
- Pitch: [noNote, L5, S3, S5, L4, S1, noNote][8].
- Rhythm+Pitch: [[gClef, noNote], [accidental sharp, L5], [accidental sharp, S3], [accidental sharp, S5], [quarter note, L4], [eight note, S1], [bar line, noNote]].

---

[7] http://www.rism.info/.

[8] L = Line; S=Space; L1 is the bottom line on the staff and S1 is the space between line 1 and 2.

Symbol Error Rate (SER). This metric is based on the well-known Word Error Rate (WER) metric [34] used in speech and text recognition. SER also uses the Levenshtein distance. The main difference between them is that the Levenshtein distance computes the differences at character level, WER does it at the word level and SER does it at symbol level. In the case of music scores, given a prediction and a reference ground-truth, the SER is defined as the minimum number of edit operation *i.e.* insertions, substitutions and deletions, to convert one array into the other.

$$SER = \frac{S + D + I}{N} \tag{3}$$

where S, D and I are the number of substitutions, deletions and insertions respectively and N is the quantity of symbols in the groundtruth. Dynamic programming is used to find the minimum value.

$$SER(i,j) = min \begin{cases} SER(i-1,j) + 1 \\ SER(i,j-1) + 1 \\ SER(i-1,j-1) + \Delta(i,j) \end{cases} \tag{4}$$

where $\Delta(i,j)$ is 0 if the symbols $predicted_i$ and $reference_j$ are the same and 1 if these symbols are different.

Output's Threshold Evaluation. A threshold is applied to decide which symbols are activated at each time step. Note that this threshold is needed because we have no knowledge about the number of symbols appearing at each time step. This threshold has been experimentally set using a grid search from 0 to 1 and step of 0.1. We have selected the combination of rhythm and pitch Error Rate as a metric to choose the best threshold. Figure 7 shows the evolution of the error rate depending on the threshold. As we can see, the best threshold is 0.5 even though 0.4 achieves similar results.

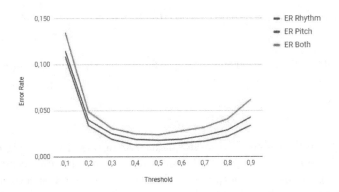

Fig. 7. Evaluation of the best threshold in terms of Error Rate: Rhythm, Pitch and Rhythm+Pitch.

4.3   Results

All the results that are shown in this section are obtained using *Adam* as optimizer with a learning rate of 10^{-4}. In this work, the PyTorch[9] library has been used in order to build the proposed framework.

Table 1 shows an error rate comparison in terms of the average and standard deviation among 5 runs. In this comparison, single directional and bidirectional LSTM are analyzed with the two described loss functions. The first column shows the loss function and the network that has been used, the second one shows the error rate of the rhythm, the third one the results concerning the pitch; and the last column shows the results when considering the rhythm and pitch jointly. Note that the BLSTM produces better results. Moreover, regarding the loss function, the Smooth L1 function obtains better results with 1.5% SER when recognizing the pitch, 2% SER when recognizing the rhythm and 2.8% SER when recognizing the pitch an rhythm jointly. Using a bidirectional network, the input is processed in both directions. Thus, it obtains information of the whole symbol, and becomes more accurate. For example, if one direction recognizes a note-head, the other direction can discard that the vertical line that it is reading is a bar line, but instead a note stem (both stems and bar lines are straight vertical lines).

Table 1. Results using LSTM and BLSTM. All results are between [0–1] given in error rate (ER). The first number is the mean of the five executions and the number between parenthesis is the standard deviation

	Rhythm (R) symbol ER	Pitch (P) symbol ER	R + P symbol ER
LSTM Smooth L1	0.326 (± 0.007)	0.293 (± 0.008)	0.426 (± 0.009)
BLSTM Smooth L1	**0.020** (± 0.001)	**0.015** (± 0.001)	**0.028** (± 0.002)
LSTM Multi Label Soft Margin	0.431 (± 0.017)	0.567 (± 0.051)	0.747 (± 0.063)
BLSTM Multi Label Soft Margin	0.027 (± 0.002)	0.023 (± 0.002)	0.036 (± 0.003)

In Figs. 8 and 9 we can see some qualitative results. First subfigure shows the input of the system. The second, third and fourth subfigures correspond to the Rhythm ground-truth, output and thresholded output respectively. In the fifth, sizth and seventh subfigures we can see the Melody ground-truth, output and thresholded output respectively.

---

[9] http://pytorch.org/.

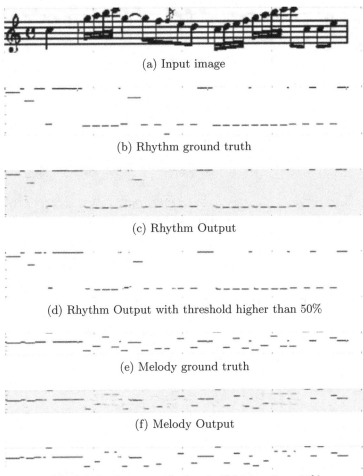

(a) Input image

(b) Rhythm ground truth

(c) Rhythm Output

(d) Rhythm Output with threshold higher than 50%

(e) Melody ground truth

(f) Melody Output

(g) Melody Output with threshold higher than 50%

Fig. 8. Qualitative results example using LSTM.

4.4   Comparison with a Commercial OMR Software

The proposed method has been compared with PhotoScore [10], a commercial OMR software able to recognize printed and also handwritten music scores. Figure 10 show qualitative results. Note that this comparison might not be completely fair. PhotoScore has some features to improve its performance that are not considered in our method. PhotoScore probably uses syntactic rules for validation. For instance, the commercial system can recognize the time signature and then validate the amount of music notes at each bar unit (which is used to solve ambiguities). Contrary, in our work, no syntactic rules have been applied.

---

[10] http://www.neuratron.com/photoscore.html.

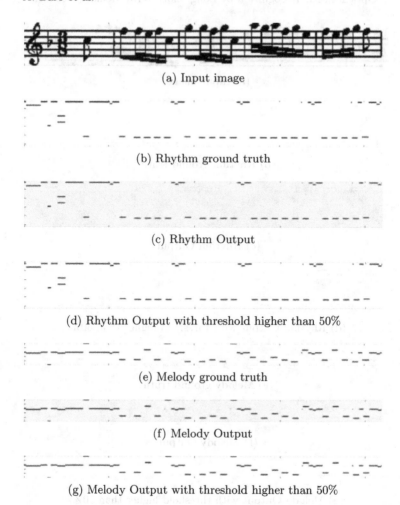

(a) Input image

(b) Rhythm ground truth

(c) Rhythm Output

(d) Rhythm Output with threshold higher than 50%

(e) Melody ground truth

(f) Melody Output

(g) Melody Output with threshold higher than 50%

Fig. 9. Qualitative results example using BLSTM.

This is an important difference because we do not correct any miss-classification using music notation rules.

Figure 10 shows that, even with a very simple music score, PhotoScore has produced two errors. First, it has confused the time of silence (5–10), and second it has added a duration dot at the end. It must be said that the method proposed in this work has correctly recognized all the music symbols.

5 Conclusion and Future Work

In this work, we have proposed an optical music recognition method that deals with single staff sheet music as a sequence making use of (B)LSTM networks.

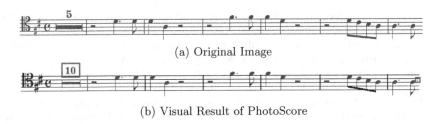

(a) Original Image

(b) Visual Result of PhotoScore

Fig. 10. Recognition of a music score using the PhotoScore Commercial OMR software. The errors are shown in red color.

The obtained results show that single staff music scores could be recognized by means of RNN. We have also shown the benefits of using a BLSTM instead of an LSTM applied to musical images. However, the recognition of scores as sequences has some limitations. For instance, more complex music scores (e.g. scores with multiple voices) require further research.

Future work will be focused on investigating transfer learning methods to recognize handwritten music scores. Moreover, we would like to incorporate musical rules or semantics as in our previous work [22] in order to solve ambiguities. In addition, we plan to investigate more suitable techniques for recognizing complex polyphonic music scores such as CNNs and attention mechanisms. In addition, we would like to convert the output of the architecture into a MIDI file, able to be listened, or to convert it into a sheet format as PhotoScore does.

Acknowledgment. This work has been partially supported by the Spanish project TIN2015-70924-C2-2-R, the Ramon y Cajal Fellowship RYC-2014-16831, the CERCA Program/Generalitat de Catalunya, FPU fellowship FPU15/06264 from the Spanish Ministerio de Educación, Cultura y Deporte, the social Sciences and Humanities Research Council of Canada and the FI fellowship AGAUR 2018 FI_B 00546 of the Generalitat de Catalunya. We gratefully acknowledge the support of NVIDIA Corporation with the donation of the Titan Xp GPU used for this research.

References

1. Rebelo, A., Fujinaga, I., Paszkiewicz, F., Marçal, A.R.S., Guedes, C., Cardoso, J.S.: Optical music recognition: state-of-the-art and open issues. IJMIR **1**(3), 173–190 (2012)
2. Bainbridge, D., Bell, T.: The challenge of optical music recognition. Comput. Hum. **35**(2), 95–121 (2001)
3. Fornés, A., Sánchez, G.: Analysis and recognition of music scores. In: Doermann, D., Tombre, K. (eds.) Handbook of Document Image Processing and Recognition, pp. 749–774. Springer, London (2014). https://doi.org/10.1007/978-0-85729-859-1_24
4. Pinto, T., Rebelo, A., Giraldi, G.A., Cardoso, J.S.: Music score binarization based on domain knowledge. Pattern Recognit. Image Anal. **2011**, 700–708 (2011)
5. Gallego, A., Calvo-Zaragoza, J.: Staff-line removal with selectional auto-encoders. Expert. Syst. Appl. **89**, 138–48 (2017)

6. Pacha, A., Eidenberger, H.: Towards a universal music symbol classifier. In: 12th International Workshop on Graphics Recognition (GREC), pp. 35–36 (2017)
7. Graves, A., Schmidhuber, J.: Offline handwriting recognition with multidimensional recurrent neural networks. In: NIPS, pp. 545–552 (2009)
8. Campos, V.B., Calvo-Zaragoza, J., Toselli, A.H., Vidal-Ruiz, E.: Sheet music statistical layout analysis. In: ICFHR, pp. 313–318 (2016)
9. Burgoyne, J.A., Ouyang, Y., Himmelman, T., Devaney, J., Pugin, L., Fujinaga, I.: Lyric extraction and recognition on digital images of early music sources. In: ISMIR, pp. 723–727 (2009)
10. Graves, A., Mohamed, A.-R., Hinton, G.: Speech recognition with deep recurrent neural networks. In: IEEE International Conference on Acoustics, Speech and Signal Processing, pp. 6645–6649. IEEE (2013)
11. Pedersoli, F., Tzanetakis, G.: Document segmentation and classification into musical scores and text. Int. J. Doc. Anal. Recognit. (IJDAR) 19(4), 289–304 (2016)
12. Fornés, A., Lladós, J., Sánchez, G., Karatzas, D.: Rotation invariant hand drawn symbol recognition based on a dynamic time warping model. IJDAR 13(3), 229–241 (2010)
13. Escalera, S., Fornés, A., Pujol, O., Radeva, P., Sánchez, G., Lladós, J.: Blurred Shape Model for binary and grey-level symbol recognition. Pattern Recognit. Lett. 30(15), 1424–1433 (2009)
14. Rebelo, A., Capela, G., Cardoso, J.S.: Optical recognition of music symbols: a comparative study. IJDAR 13(1), 19–31 (2010)
15. Rebelo, A., Tkaczuk, J., Sousa, R., Cardoso, J.S.: Metric learning for music symbol recognition. In: 2011 10th International Conference on Machine Learning and Applications and Workshops, vol. 2, pp. 106–111, December 2011
16. Coüasnon, B., Rétif, B.: Using a grammar for a reliable full score recognition system. In: ICMC (1995)
17. Pugin, L.: Optical music recognitoin of early typographic prints using hidden markov models. In: ISMIR (2006)
18. Pugin, L., Burgoyne, J.A., Fujinaga, I.: Map adaptation to improve optical music recognition of early music documents using hidden markov models. In: ISMIR (2007)
19. Pinto, J.C., Vieira, P., Sousa, J.M.: A new graph-like classification method applied to ancient handwritten musical symbols. Doc. Anal. Recognit. 6(1), 10–22 (2003)
20. Choi, K.-Y., Coüasnon, B., Ricquebourg, Y., Zanibbi, R.: Bootstrapping samples of accidentals in dense piano scores for CNN-based detection. In: 12th International Workshop on Graphics Recognition (GREC), pp. 19–20 (2017)
21. Dorfer, M., Hajič, J., Widmer, G.: On the potential of fully convolutional neural networks for musical symbol detection. In: 12th International Workshop on Graphics Recognition (GREC), pp. 53–54 (2017)
22. Baró, A., Riba, P., Fornés, A.: Towards the recognition of compound music notes in handwritten music scores. In: ICFHR, pp. 465–470, October 2016
23. Matsushima, T., Ohteru, S., Hashimoto, S.: An integrated music information processing system: PSB-er. In: Proceedings of the International Computer Music Conference, pp. 191–198 (1989)
24. Goodfellow, I., Bengio, Y., Courville, A.: Deep Learning. MIT Press (2016). http://www.deeplearningbook.org
25. Owens, A., Isola, P., McDermott, J.H., Torralba, A., Adelson, E.H., Freeman, W.T.: Visually indicated sounds. CoRR, vol. abs/1512.08512 (2015)
26. Aytar, Y., Vondrick, C., Torralba, A.: SoundNet: learning sound representations from unlabeled video. CoRR, vol. abs/1610.09001 (2016)

27. Sübakan, Y.C., Smaragdis, P.: Diagonal RNNs in symbolic music modeling. CoRR, vol. abs/1704.05420 (2017)
28. Kalingeri, V., Grandhe, S.: Music generation with deep learning. CoRR, vol. abs/1612.04928 (2016)
29. Pascanu, R., Gülçehre, Ç., Cho, K., Bengio, Y.: How to construct deep recurrent neural networks. CoRR, vol. abs/1312.6026 (2013)
30. van der Wel, E., Ullrich, K.: Optical music recognition with convolutional sequence-to-sequence models. CoRR, vol. abs/1707.04877 (2017)
31. Calvo-Zaragoza, J., Valero-Mas, J.J., Pertusa, A.: End-to-end optical music recognition using neural networks. In: ISMIR (2017)
32. Pacha, A., Eidenberger, H.M.: Towards self-learning optical music recognition. In: 2017 16th IEEE International Conference on Machine Learning and Applications (ICMLA), pp. 795–800 (2017)
33. Hochreiter, S., Schmidhuber, J.: Long short-term memory. Neural Comput. **9**, 1735–1780 (1997)
34. Frinken, V., Bunke, H.: Continuous handwritten script recognition. In: Doermann, D., Tombre, K. (eds.) Handbook of Document Image Processing and Recognition, pp. 391–425. Springer, London (2014). https://doi.org/10.1007/978-0-85729-859-1_12

Interpretation of Engineering Drawings and Maps

Extracting Information from Molecular Pathway Diagrams

Antonio Foncubierta-Rodríguez[(⊠)], Anca-Nicoleta Ciubotaru, Costas Bekas, and Maria Gabrani

IBM Research Zurich, Rüschlikon, Switzerland
fra@zurich.ibm.com

Abstract. Health and life sciences' research fields like personalized medicine, drug discovery, pharmacovigilance and systems biology make an intensive use of graphical information to represent knowledge in the form of domain-specific diagrams, such as molecular pathway's. The aim is to provide added value to written text in scientific literature and related documents. Enabling access to all the existing literature for further research requires enabling access to the information contained in these diagrams. Molecular pathways are very different from more conventional diagrams (e.g. flowcharts), and therefore interpretation of molecular pathway diagrams requires domain-specific knowledge to remove ambiguity. In this paper, we propose a method that automatically extracts information from molecular pathways using computer vision techniques. To the best of our knowledge this is the first attempt to retrieve information from images depicting molecular pathway diagrams. The lack of a significant, publicly available dataset with annotated ground truth has led to experimental evaluation on synthetic data. Results show high precision and recall values for the detection of entities and relations. We compare and describe the substantial differences between the proposed method and prior art on the closest diagram type using CLEF-IP flowchart summarization task.

1 Introduction

Science is a cumulative task, where new knowledge is always built upon prior knowledge [1]. Scientific production, in the form of conference proceedings, presentations and journal articles is constantly growing. This information overload requires updated computer-based tools to make knowledge accessible and, most importantly, searchable and interpretable. The goal of making information accessible and reusable for future research, requires understanding not only text but also graphical information [2].

Specific fields, including personalized medicine, drug discovery, pharmacovigilance and systems biology make intensive use of graphical information to provide added value to written text in scientific publications. Molecular pathway diagrams are one major tool used by scientists aiming at summarizing, describing and representing complex relations between various biological entities. The term *molecular pathway* is used in this paper as a common denomination of metabolic

© Springer Nature Switzerland AG 2018
A. Fornés and B. Lamiroy (Eds.): GREC 2017, LNCS 11009, pp. 99–114, 2018.
https://doi.org/10.1007/978-3-030-02284-6_8

pathways, signal transduction pathways, regulatory networks or genetic pathways, among others. In general, a molecular pathway diagram is a graphical representation of any actions, changes, relations and interactions between the phenotype of a living organism, genes, RNA, proteins, drugs or other molecules.

Molecular pathway diagrams contain extremely valuable information for researchers that is integrated into searchable databases [3,4]. These databases are built with the assistance of experts that manually curate [5–7] each of the relations that are included in the database, often combining text mining on published sources [8] and additional tools for discovery [9], conflict-resolution [10] and integration [11,12]. However, these tools neglect the information that is contained in the images that accompany the publications.

Figure 1 contains a selection of molecular pathway diagrams extracted from the literature, demonstrating the enormous heterogeneity within the molecular pathways category and why initiatives like the Systems Biology Graphical Notation (SBGN) [13] and the Systems Biology Markup Language (SBML) [14] will provide a more stable framework for designing and interpreting these diagrams when the related standards are mature. In fact, the use of molecular pathways in scientific literature to describe molecular-level interactions is quite recent. A well-established initiative like the modality classification task of Image-CLEF [15] does not contain a specific class for molecular pathways in their modality hierarchy [16]. Methods designed to identify the various modalities of graphs and diagrams found in documents are extremely helpful in case of similarity based retrieval [17], but they are only the first step in addressing the extraction of domain-specific information. In this paper we describe a method that extracts molecular pathway information from raster images of these diagrams. The proposed method uses image analysis and a cognitive model to extract entity-relation information from diagrams through reasoning and automatically produces a structured textual version of the content, opening the possibility to obtain comprehensive knowledge based on several documents.

The rest of the paper is organized as follows: in Sect. 2 we review the state of the art in extracting information from diagrams, analyzing related work on the closest types of diagrams. In Sect. 3 we present the domain-specific characteristics of molecular pathway diagrams and how they differ from other types of diagrams. In Sect. 4 we describe the main principles of the framework and how they are used to extract molecular interactions. We evaluate the effectiveness and performance of the proposed method using the data described in Sect. 5 and we discuss the results in Sect. 6. We conclude the paper with our planned with future work in Sect. 7.

2   Related Work

Analysis of graphical information from documents can be performed at various scales. Going from the largest to the finest scale we can, among other tasks, classify complete images and graphs into predefined categories, localize and annotate specific objects, or extract structured information from diagrams. The idea behind information extraction from diagrams is to build a cognitive model based on computer vision and artificial intelligence that is able to describe all the relevant content in the image.

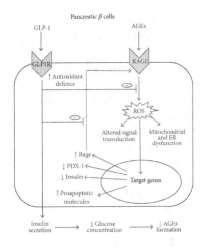

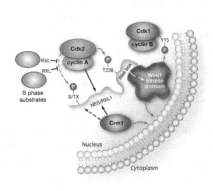

(a) Molecular pathway showing various interaction types. Source: [18]

(b) Molecular pathway combined with a drawing of the membrane between cell and cytoplasm. Source: [19]

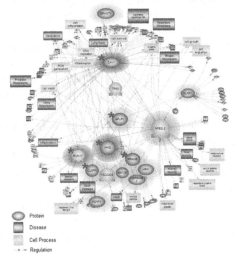

(c) Molecular pathway with occluded entities and relations. Source: [20]

Fig. 1. Examples of molecular pathway diagrams from various sources, showing the heterogeneity of this type of diagrams.

The earliest theoretical discussions on information extraction from diagrams occurred in the 1990s [21,22] and although to the best of our knowledge none of the existing approaches deals with the specificities of molecular pathway diagrams (see Sect. 3), we have reviewed the most relevant state of the art for diagram understanding. Target applications range from UML (Unified Modeling Language) diagrams [23–25], flowcharts [26–28], military action plans [29] or electrical diagrams [30,31].

Nakamura et al. [32] proposed natural language to improve the understanding of diagrams, but there is no automated effort in the detection of lines, shapes or other graphical items; and the processing of all this information is done by humans. Butler et al. [33] define a formal framework to retrieve information from data flow diagrams. Implementation details are not discussed, and their most important contribution is a formalism to encode data flow diagrams as a set of tuples. Watanabe and Nagao [34] apply natural language methods to plant description drawings, without interpretation of the graphical elements.

In [23], Lank et al. proposed a system to recognize UML diagrams on an electronic white board, making use of the user interaction as part of the input to recognize individual elements. Similarly, Forbus et al. [29] use sketch-based visual reasoning and gestures to digitalize battle plans of the US military. Other methods relying on user interaction are [24,25,30,31].

The closest related work is the flowchart summarization task organized during The Cross Language Evaluation Forum (CLEF) in 2012. In this evaluation campaign, three participants submitted their methods to summarize the content of flowchart diagrams extracted from patent documents. All three participants use variations of the same approach, which consists in separating text from graphical elements and then classify boxes and edges. Mözinger et al. [35] use a combination of binary operations (thinning, closing and opening) to separate characters from line segments. Rusiñol et al. divide the image in a graphical, a textual and an undefined layer. Then they perform detection of specific symbols to find the nodes [36]. A similar approach is followed by Thean et al. [26], who also investigated the use of various OCR methods.

To the best of our knowledge, the method we present in this paper is the first to propose fully automated understanding of molecular pathway diagrams. By using computer vision and machine learning we aim to extract structured information from raster images that can be incorporated into databases or converted to textual summaries using natural language generation.

In the next section we describe the specificities of this type of diagram, and explain why extracting information from molecular pathways needs to be addressed with a tool that is designed with this specificities in mind.

3   Specificities of Molecular Pathways

Enclosing shapes. Due to the ongoing standardization effort for molecular pathways, there is not a fixed definition of what are the valid enclosing shapes for the entities. This forces any information extraction approach to be as general as possible in terms of shape expectation and detection and not rely exclusively on a fixed set of known shapes, such as ellipses, rectangles, etc.

Occlusion. The information density in a molecular pathway can be extremely high, as shown in Fig. 1c. Occlusion is, therefore, a major problem during the analysis of these diagrams and specific measures need to be taken in order to extract information. There are two types of possible occlusions: entity-level occlusion and relation-level occlusion.

Entities and interaction types. Molecular pathways often represent various types of interactions between several types of entities. Figure 2 shows the possible entities and interactions in a hierarchical way. These entity and relation subtypes are represented in various ways using graphical representations. e.g. it is common to describe a protein inhibition using an arrow with a T-shaped head.

Hypothetical interactions and entities Although the SBGN initiative recommends using dashed or dotted lines to represent hypothetical interactions, the truth is that many authors rely on color, line thickness or even text attributes to provide this information.

Resolution and OCR. Space limitations in scientific publications force many authors to reduce the resolution of diagrams to stay within the page limits. This, along with the dense knowledge representation often witnessed at molecular pathways, has a severe impact on OCR (Optical Character Recognition) of the entities, but also on the recognition of relations.

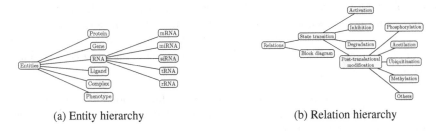

(a) Entity hierarchy   (b) Relation hierarchy

Fig. 2. Hierarchical classification of entities and relations frequently found in molecular pathways.

4   A Comprehensive Model for Diagrams Applied to Molecular Pathways

The principle of our method is to extract basic objects in the diagram, such as characters and line segments (see Sect. 4.1), and then through reasoning, construct structural primitives, such as texts and information carrying shapes (see Sect. 4.2), that can be labeled with their actual semantic meaning in the context of the diagram. This cognitive approach is summarized in Fig. 3. The reason why we use this approach is that, by progressively moving from lower level features to higher level structural and semantic information, the methodology can be adapted to cover as much of the heterogeneity as possible within a specific domain, but also it allows to use the same procedure for extracting information from generic diagrams such as line, scatter or bubble plots.

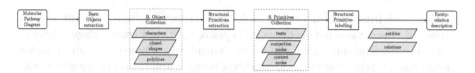

Fig. 3. Overview of the information extraction pipeline together with the type of outputs generated at each step.

4.1 Basic Object Detection

Given the existing heterogeneity in the molecular pathway diagrams extracted from the scientific literature, the first step in the pipeline of the proposed method has the goal to reduce all the possible graphical elements into the three categories that carry most of the information: characters, polylines and closed shapes. It is obvious that other primitives might be present in the diagrams, e.g. drawings, shadings, and color information. In the current implementation of the proposed method these primitives are not used to extract specific information, but are compatible with the system: e.g. color information is part of the preprocessing and binarization process, but with no further implication in reasoning.

After preprocessing and applying a learned threshold, the connected components of the binary image are classified according to the following context-based reasoning:

- Characters are the most frequent single basic object type. Therefore a threshold for characters is defined using the mode of the distribution of height and width of connected components.
- Background areas surrounded by a single connected component are relevant closed shapes if they contain characters, otherwise they are considered loops formed by edges.
- Every other connected component that is not text or a closed shape is part of a polyline describing one or multiple edges, since there might be intersections.

These rules lead to a simplified version of the diagram, containing only the basic objects.

4.2 Structural Primitives Resolution

Once the individual basic objects have been found, the structure of the diagram is inferred building structural primitives which contain higher level information about the basic objects. The idea is to obtain structural information that can, in the next step, be labeled as entity, relation, or an attribute of any of them.

Extracting texts out of characters Groups of characters are clustered together using mathematical morphology and a structuring element of the same size as the average character. A dilation operation on the image of the characters with such a structuring element produces text blobs that work as a mask for text locations. Each of these text blobs are extracted independently and processed using Tesseract OCR [37]. Since the character detection is simply based on the size of the connected components, OCR recognition confidence is used to discard noise.

Connection Nodes Detection. Connection nodes are the singular points of a polyline: intersections with other lines and objects, abrupt changes in curvature and endpoints of the polyline. In order to identify the connection nodes we perform corner detection using the Harris and Stephens algorithm [38] separately on each independent polyline. As it can be seen in Fig. 4 there are several pixels that produce a high response to the corner detection for each actual connection node. To resolve this ambiguity we propose the use of the same principle as explained for character grouping: dilation using an image-dependent structuring element. We then apply this as a mask to find the center of mass of the actual connection point.

Defining Content Nodes. Molecular pathways often contain text that is enclosed by ellipses, rectangles and other shapes, but it is not infrequent to observe texts that are not enclosed. We use the information from both the closed shapes basic objects and the text structural primitives to produce a partition of the image space that identifies the position of the closest content node. We achieve this by using a distance transform on a map that contains the texts and shapes bounding boxes. We next create a Voronoi diagram where we can assign an identification number to each region with relevant content.

4.3   Labeled Structural Primitives

The final step consists of labeling the relevant structural primitives so that entities and relations can be obtained. Entities are labeled using all the text included in each Voronoi region (see Fig. 5). The relations are constructed by labeling each of the connection nodes as either endpoint (e.g. the start or end of an arrow in a directed edge) or as intersection point. Intersection points are resolved so that the actual path is recovered. The relation resolution process is performed using a rule-based reasoning exploiting structural primitive-generated features as follows:

1. Construct a list where the i-th element represents the nodes that are connected to it.
2. Pairs of nodes that are connected to each other only are defined as a relation between the Voronoi regions where the connection nodes are located.
3. If one node i is connected to a node j, but this node connects to several other nodes, the j-th node is labeled as a connection node and a next-node resolution algorithm is started:
   (a) The polyline segment connecting node i and j is analyzed to compute the predominant direction as a vector $\mathbf{v}_{ij}$.
   (b) The rest of polyline segments connecting node j with other nodes k_j are used to define $\mathbf{v}_{jk_j}$.

(c) The next node for the path is chosen as the one with a largest absolute value of the normalized scalar product:

$$\left|\frac{\mathbf{v_{ij}}\mathbf{v_{jk_j}}}{|\mathbf{v_{ij}}||\mathbf{v_{jk_j}}|}\right| = \left|cos(\angle(\mathbf{v_{ij}}, \mathbf{v_{jk_j}}))\right|.$$

The maximum value is 1 when the two vectors point in the same direction and the minimum is 0 if they are orthogonal.

4. When all paths are defined, the amount of foreground pixels in the neighborhood of the end nodes are checked to define the directionality of the edge. The relation is labeled as directed if the ratio of foreground pixels in the neighborhood of each of the endpoints of the path is above a experimentally learned threshold. In that case, the direction goes from the entity in the Voronoi region with fewer foreground pixels to the entity in the Voronoi region with a larger amount.

(a) Binary image of the diagram.

(b) P. Image representing an arrow shape (polyline basic object) connecting two nodes.

(c) $H(P \oplus S)$. Response to Harris and Stephens corner detection algorithm on the dilated version of P with a structuring element S.

(d) $M = \max(H(P \oplus S))$. Local maxima of the response to the corner detection algorithm.

(e) $N = (M \oplus S)(P \oplus S)$. Endnodes are detected by masking the dilated polyline with the dilated maxima of the corner detection.

Fig. 4. Detection of connection points in a polyline.

5   Dataset

The basic goal of the proposed method is to obtain information from molecular pathways found in the scientific literature, since it is not part of the textual content of the document. This poses an obvious challenge in the evaluation phase, since there is no ground truth available.

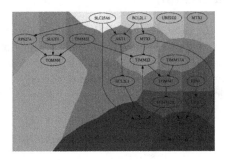

Fig. 5. Use of Voronoi diagram to label entities according to structural primitives

During the design of the method we downloaded 9938 articles from PubMED Central[1], using the queries "molecular pathway" and "regulatory network". Images from these publications were manually reviewed and 451 molecular pathways were found. They were classified as follows:

- 123 of them contained molecular pathways with default characteristics (grayscale or color images, with closed shapes, texts and continuous lines representing relations, as seen Fig. 9).
- 159 of them contained the default characteristics and additional drawings e.g. cell membranes, mitochondria, etc (see Fig. 1b).
- 82 of them contained the default characteristics and dashed lines to represent hypothetical relations or entities.
- 87 of them contained the default characteristics and severely occluded entities or relations where text was not readable (see Fig. 1c).

According to this distribution, we decided to generate an annotated dataset following the assumptions of the default group. Using a directed graph generation tool commonly used for generating molecular pathways in the literature, we generated synthetic diagrams using existing protein names using information from the structured databases that contain curated pathways, various shapes, randomly connected to each other, with various arrow shapes and also at varying resolutions. Figure 6 shows an example of one of the diagrams generated. In the current evaluation pipeline, the only sources of noise included were the JPEG compression artifacts and resolution.

---

[1] https://www.ncbi.nlm.nih.gov/pmc/, as of March 2018.

The dataset of synthetic diagrams containing protein names consists of 1000 images with up to 25 nodes and entities. In order to address the impact of resolution, number of nodes and number of entities separately, a second dataset containing 800 images was generated. This dataset does not contain protein names, in order to remove dependency on OCR recognition.

6   Experimental Results

Evaluation of correct detection is based on the following aspects: entities are correctly detected only if the text is spelled exactly as in the ground truth. Changes in number of white spaces or casing yields an incorrect detection. Relations are correctly detected only if the involved entities are correct. Therefore precision of OCR in entity detection affects the maximum precision of relation detection.

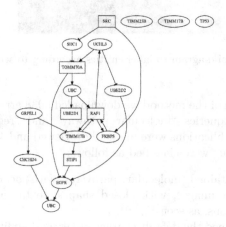

Fig. 6. Synthetic molecular pathway diagram generated using random shapes and protein names

Table 1 contains the results of the detection of entities and relations using the synthetic dataset generated with protein names. Table 2 shows the precision and recall obtained for entity and relation detection. Comparison between Tables 1 and 2 clearly shows the impact of OCR recognition. By relaxing the way we evaluate the metrics the values could be significantly larger, but since the correct detection of entities is of significant semantic value, we keep them very strict, with the relevant effects in our performance values.

The impact of image resolution is shown in Fig. 7 where we evaluate the performance for two resolutions, namely 100 dpi and 200 dpi, both smaller than the minimal printing resolution of 300 dpi. Resolution does not appear to have a strong effect on the recognition of relations. If any, it has a slight effect in the detection of entities, that is the performance of OCR. This is expected since OCR is based on closed object detection.

Table 1. Precision and recall on a synthetic dataset of 1000 molecular pathway diagrams with existing protein names.

	Precision	Recall
Entity detection	0.73	0.74
Relation detection	0.50	0.54
Directed relation detection	0.49	0.52

Table 2. Precision and recall on a synthetic dataset of 800 randomly generated molecular pathways.

	Precision	Recall
Entity detection	0.96	0.97
Relation detection	0.85	0.84
Directed relation detection	0.82	0.79

Knowledge density, represented by the number of entities and relations in the diagram, has proven to be the most important problem in the recognition of relations as shown in Fig. 8. This is expected, because density affects both complexity in data and structural representation.

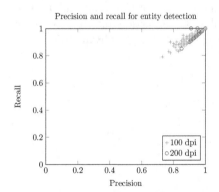

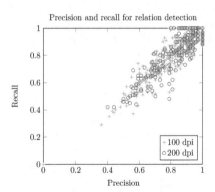

(a) Results of entity detection. Average precision and recall are 0.96 and 0.97.

(b) Results of relation detection. Average precision and recall are 0.85 and 0.84.

Fig. 7. Results of entity and relation detection in dataset of 800 randomly generated molecular pathways grouped by image resolution.

Although real data extracted from scientific papers cannot be used for exhaustive quantitative tests due to the lack of ground truth, we include in Fig. 9 an example of a real diagram that was analyzed using the proposed method and the correctly identified entities and relations. The figure has a significant number

Precision and recall for entity detection

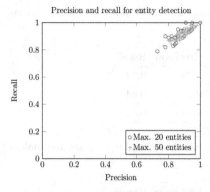

Precision and recall for relation detection

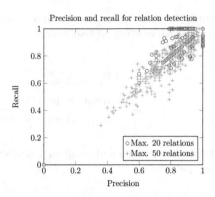

(a) Results of entity detection. Average precision and recall are 0.96 and 0.97.

(b) Results of relation detection. Average precision and recall are 0.85 and 0.84.

Fig. 8. Results of entity and relation detection in dataset of 800 randomly generated molecular pathways grouped by maximum number of entities and relations.

of entities (66) and relations (63) and numerous challenges, such as occlusions, different representations of both entities and relations and low resolution. Results show that even in this challenging case, our method was able to detect correctly 83% of the entities and 38% of the relations.

With respect to the closest related work, which is the flowchart summarization task of CLEF-IP in 2012, the proposed method performs on molecular pathway diagrams similarly to the reported results of the participants [26,35,36] on flowcharts. The reported structural level accuracy (omitting OCR and direction-

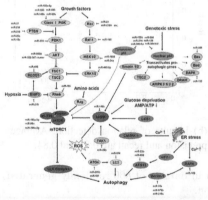

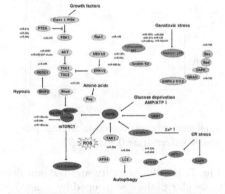

(a) Original molecular pathway containing 66 distinct entities and 63 relations

(b) Correctly identified entities (83%) and relations (38%) using the proposed method.

Fig. 9. Results of extracting information from a molecular pathway extracted from scientific literature [39].

ality) in the CLEF-IP task ranges between 0.86 to 0.90, which is slightly lower than the values obtained in our experiments (summarized in Table 3), illustrating the power of the proposed method. Moreover, the scenario of molecular pathways that we address is much more heterogeneous: e.g. there is no sink/source concept to represent a flow direction, there are not predefined shapes to train on, the use of curves and intersecting lines is frequent.

Table 3. Results compared to CLEF-IP 2012 Flowchart summarization task according to [36].

Approach	Avg. Recall
Rusiñol et al. [36]	0.90
Thean et al. [26]	0.88
Mörzinger et al. [35]	0.86
Proposed (20 entities, 20 relations)	**0.94**
Proposed (20 entities, 50 relations)	0.83
Proposed (50 entities, 20 relations)	**0.94**
Proposed (50 entities, 50 relations)	**0.96**

7   Conclusions and Future Work

In this article we present a domain-specific method to extract information from scientific diagrams following the principles of using basic objects, structural primitives and semantic reasoning. Quantitative results show the impact of OCR as a limitation factor of information extraction pipeline. With OCR effects removed, we studied the effect of knowledge density and resolution. Precision and recall values are close to 0.95 for entities and 0.80–0.85 for undirected and directed relations on 100 and 200 dpi resolution images, while the minimal printer resolution is 300 dpi.

Correct detection of relations between entities has been proven more difficult than detection of entities themselves. In this paper we modelled reasoning with a rules-based approach. We plan next to build reasoning through a Probabilistic Graphical Model, in order to infer what are the correct relations based on the labeled structural primitives and features computed on them.

Finally, we believe that the work described in this article shows a path for future research that will enable access to all types of information contained in scientific and related documents.

References

1. Brocke, J.V., et al.: Reconstructing the giant: On the importance of rigour in documenting the literature search process. In: ECIS Proceedings (2009)
2. Müller, H., Foncubierta-Rodríguez, A., Lin, C., Eggel, I.: Determining the importance of figures in journal articles to find representative images. In: SPIE Proceedings, vol. 8674 (2013)
3. Fabregat, A., et al.: The reactome pathway knowledgebase. Nucleic Acids Res. **44**(D1), D481–D487 (2016)
4. Petri, V., et al.: The pathway ontology - updates and applications. J. Biomed. Semant. **5**(1), 7 (2014)
5. Davis, A.P., et al.: The comparative toxicogenomics database: update 2011. Nucleic Acids Res. **39**(Database issue), D1067–D1072 (2011)
6. Hayman, G.T., et al.: The updated RGD pathway portal utilizes increased curation efficiency and provides expanded pathway information. Hum. Genomics **7**, 4 (2013)
7. Paley, S.M., Latendresse, M., Karp, P.D.: Regulatory network operations in the pathway tools software. BMC Bioinformatics **13**, 243 (2012)
8. Ravikumar, K.E., Wagholikar, K.B., Liu, H.: Challenges in adapting text mining for full text articles to assist pathway curation. In: Proceedings of the 5th ACM Conference on Bioinformatics, Computational Biology, and Health Informatics, BCB 2014, pp. 551–558. ACM, New York (2014)
9. García-Jiménez, B., Pons, T., Sanchis, A., Valencia, A.: Predicting protein relationships to human pathways through a relational learning approach based on simple sequence features. IEEE/ACM Trans. Comput. Biol. Bioinform. **11**(4), 753–765 (2014)
10. Yoon, S., et al.: Systematic identification of context-dependent conflicting information in biological pathways. In: Proceedings of the ACM 8th International Workshop on Data and Text Mining in Bioinformatics, DTMBIO 2014, p. 9. ACM, New York (2014)
11. Luna, A., Sunshine, M.L., van Iersel, M.P., Aladjem, M.I., Kohn, K.W.: PathVisio-MIM: Pathvisio plugin for creating and editing molecular interaction maps (MIMs). Bioinformatics **27**(15), 2165–2166 (2011)
12. Wang, Y.T., Huang, Y.H., Chen, Y.C., Hsu, C.L., Yang, U.C.: PINT: pathways integration tool. Nucleic Acids Res. **38**(Web Server issue), W124–W131 (2010)
13. Le Novere, N., et al.: The systems biology graphical notation, **27**(8) 735–741
14. Hucka, M., et al.: The systems biology markup language (SBML): a medium for representation and exchange of biochemical network models, **19**(4), 524–531
15. Garcia Seco de Herrera, A., Kalpathy-Cramer, J., Demner-Fushman, D., Antani, S., Müller, H.: Overview of the ImageCLEF 2013 medical tasks. In: CLEF (Working Notes) (2013)
16. Müller, H., Kalpathy-Cramer, J., Demner-Fushman, D., Antani, S.: Creating a classification of image types in the medical literature for visual categorization. In: Proceedings SPIE 8319, Medical Imaging 2012: Advanced PACS-based Imaging Informatics and Therapeutic Applications, vol. 8319, pp. 83190P–83190P-12 (2012)
17. Foncubierta-Rodríguez, A., García Seco de Herrerea, A. Müller, H.: Medical image retrieval using bag of meaningful visual words: unsupervised visual vocabulary pruning with PLSA. In: Proceedings of the 1st ACM International Workshop on Multimedia Indexing and Information Retrieval for Healthcare, MIIRH 2013, pp. 75–82. ACM (2013)

18. Puddu, A., Mach, F., Nencioni, A., Viviani, G.L., Montecucco, F.: An Emerging Role of Glucagon-Like Peptide-1 in Preventing Advanced-Glycation-End-Product-Mediated Damages in Diabetes. Mediators of Inflammation 2013 (2013)
19. Enders, G.H.: Gauchos and ochos: a Wee1-Cdk tango regulating mitotic entry. Cell Div. **5**, 12 (2010)
20. Kim, H.L., Seo, Y.R.: Molecular and genomic approach for understanding the gene-environment interaction between Nrf2 deficiency and carcinogenic nickel-induced DNA damage. Oncol. Rep. **28**(6), 1959–1967 (2012)
21. Futrelle, R.P.: Strategies for diagram understanding: generalized equivalence, spatial/object pyramids and animate vision. In: Proceedings of the Conference on 10th International Pattern Recognition, vol. 1, pp. 403–408 (1990)
22. Futrelle, R.P., Kakadiaris, I.A., Alexander, J., Carriero, C.M., Nikolakis, N., Futrelle, J.M.: Understanding diagrams in technical documents. Computer **25**(7), 75–78 (1992)
23. Lank, E., Thorley, J., Chen, S., Blostein, D.: On-line recognition of UML diagrams. In: Proceedings of Sixth International Conference on Document Analysis and Recognition, Institute of Electrical & Electronics Engineers (IEEE) (2001)
24. Zheng, W.T., Sun, Z.X.: Knowledge-based hierarchical sketch understanding. In: Proceedings of International Conference Machine Learning and Cybernetics, vol. 5, pp. 2838–2843, August 2005
25. Hammond, T., Davis, R.: Tahuti: a geometrical sketch recognition system for UML class diagrams. In: ACM SIGGRAPH 2006 Courses, SIGGRAPH 2006. ACM, New York (2006)
26. Thean, A., Deltorn, J.M., Lopez, P., Romary, L.: Textual summarisation of flowcharts in patent drawings for CLEF-IP 2012. In: CLEF 2012 (2012)
27. Lupu, M., Piroi, F., Hanbury, A.: Evaluating flowchart recognition for patent retrieval. In: EVIA@ NTCIR (2013)
28. Rusiñol, M., de las Heras, L.P., Terrades, O.R.: Flowchart recognition for non-textual information retrieval in patent search. Inf. Retrieval **17**(5-6), 545–562 (2014)
29. Forbus, K.D., Usher, J., Chapman, V.: Sketching for military courses of action diagrams. In: Proceedings of the 8th International Conference on Intelligent User Interfaces, IUI 2003, pp. 61–68. ACM, New York (2003)
30. Mas, J., Sanchez, G., Llados, J., Lamiroy, B.: An incremental on-line parsing algorithm for recognizing sketching diagrams. In: Ninth International Conference on Document Analysis and Recognition (ICDAR 2007), Institute of Electrical & Electronics Engineers (IEEE), September 2007
31. Feng, G., Viard-Gaudin, C., Sun, Z.: On-line hand-drawn electric circuit diagram recognition using 2D dynamic programming. Pattern Recogn. **42**(12), 3215–3223 (2009)
32. Nakamura, Y., Furukawa, R., Nagao, M.: Diagram understanding utilizing natural language text. In: Proceedings of Second International Document Analysis and Recognition Conference, pp. 614–618, October 1993
33. Butler, G., Grogono, P., Shinghal, R., Tjandra, I.: Retrieving information from data flow diagrams. In: Proceedings of 2nd Working Conference Reverse Engineering, pp. 22–29, July 1995
34. Watanabe, Y., Nagao, M.: Diagram understanding using integration of layout information and textual information. In: Proceedings of the 17th International Conference on Computational Linguistics, COLING 1998, vol. 2, pp. 1374–1380. Association for Computational Linguistics, Stroudsburg (1998)

35. Mörzinger, R., Schuster, R., Horti, A., Thallinger, G.: Visual structure analysis of flow charts in patent images. In: CLEF (Online Working Notes/Labs/Workshop) (2012)
36. Rusiñol, M., et al.: CVC-UAB's participation in the flowchart recognition task of CLEF-IP 2012. In: CLEF (Online Working Notes/Labs/Workshop) (2012)
37. Smith, R.: An overview of the Tesseract OCR engine. In: Proceedings of the Ninth International Conference on Document Analysis and Recognition, ICDAR 2007, vol. 02, pp. 629–633. IEEE Computer Society, Washington, DC (2007)
38. Harris, C., Stephens, M.: A combined corner and edge detector. In: Alvey Vision Conference, vol. 15, p. 50. Citeseer (1988)
39. Su, Z., Yang, Z., Xu, Y., Chen, Y., Yu, Q.: MicroRNAs in apoptosis, autophagy and necroptosis. Oncotarget 6(11), 8474–8490 (2015)

Extraction of Ancient Map Contents Using Trees of Connected Components

Jordan Drapeau[1(✉)], Thierry Géraud[3(✉)], Mickaël Coustaty[1(✉)],
Joseph Chazalon[1,3(✉)], Jean-Christophe Burie[1(✉)], Véronique Eglin[2(✉)],
and Stéphane Bres[2(✉)]

[1] Laboratoire L3i, University of La Rochelle, 17042 La Rochelle Cedex 1, France
{jordan.drapeau,mickael.coustaty,joseph.chazalon,
jean-christophe.burie}@univ-lr.fr
[2] Université de Lyon, CNRS, INSA-Lyon, LIRIS, UMR5205, 69621 Lyon, France
{veronique.eglin,stephane.bres}@insa-lyon.fr
[3] EPITA Research and Development Laboratory (LRDE), Le Kremlin-Bicetre,
France
{thierry.geraud,joseph.chazalon}@lrde.epita.fr

Abstract. Ancient maps are an historical and cultural heritage widely recognized as a very important source of information, especially for dialectological researches, the cartographical heritage produces first-rate data. However, exploiting such maps is a quite difficult task to achieve, and we are focusing our attention on this major issue. In this paper, we consider the Linguistic Atlas of France (ALF), built between 1902 and 1910 and we propose an original approach using tree of connected components for the separation of the content in layers for facilitating the extraction, the analysis, the viewing and the diffusion of the data contained in these ancient linguistic atlases.

Keywords: Mathematical morphology · Connected components
Map analysis · Text/Graphics separation · Linguistic Atlas

1 Introduction

Ancient maps are a historical and cultural heritage widely recognized as a very important source of information, but not easy to use. In this paper, we are focusing on the Linguistic Atlas of France (ALF), which is a collection of maps in paper format[1]. It comprises 35 booklets, bringing together in 12 volumes, 1920 geolinguistic maps presenting an instantaneous picture of the dialect situation of France at the end of the 19th century. It can be defined as a first-generation atlas publishing raw data and constituting a corpus of more than one million of reliable lexical data, homogeneously transcribed, using the Rousselot-Gilliéron phonetic alphabet.

---

[1] Dataset available at http://lig-tdcge.imag.fr/cartodialect3/carteTheme.

A. Fornés and B. Lamiroy (Eds.): GREC 2017, LNCS 11009, pp. 115–130, 2018.
https://doi.org/10.1007/978-3-030-02284-6_9

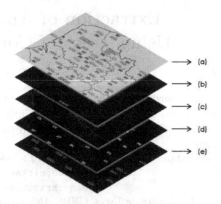

Fig. 1. Left: A French department name in red, a survey point number in blue, and a word in phonetics in green. Right: (a) Map; (b) French departments names; (c) Borders; (d) Survey point numbers; (e) Words in phonetics. (Color figure online)

The ALF maps are mainly composed of three kinds of elements: names of French departments (always surrounded by a rectangle), survey point numbers (identification of a city where a survey has been done), and words in phonetics (pronunciation of the word written in Rousselot-Gilliéron phonetic alphabet). Let us note that each map gathers the different pronunciations of a given word into a single map. An illustration of these components is given in Fig. 1.

This atlas is of prime interest for the researchers in dialectology as it allows to understand how the French language has evolved over the last century. This work takes place in the context of the ECLATS project, a French national research project[2] which aims at automatically extracting this information and generating maps with selected elements (currently, this process is done manually and it takes weeks to build a single map). More specifically, the aim of this paper is to separate each kind of information into layers in order to prepare data for subsequent analysis. The different layers of information are shown in Fig. 1 (right).

2   Related Work

Maps are composed of different layers of informations. Decomposing an image into meaningful components appears as one of major aims in recent development in image processing. The first goal was image restoration and denoising; but following the ideas of Meyer [17], in total variation minimization framework of Rudin, Osher and Fatemi [18], image decomposition into geometrical and oscillatory (i.e., texture) components appears an useful and very interesting way in computer vision and image analysis. There is a very large literature and also

2 This work is supported by the French National Research Agency under the grant number ANR-15-CE38-0002.

recent advances on image decomposition models, image regularization, texture extraction and modeling or text-graphic separation. Among all the methods that have been proposed in the litterature, we can easily identify three main categories.

The first category of layer decomposition was based on color information. Color-based approaches have been used for separating an image into many layers [2,8,10] by clustering the color present in the document/map. However, the maps from our project can be seen as black and white images (black and white edited documents, worn out by time, then scanned, which makes them grayer and yellower) and layers of informations can not be distinguished using colors.

Looking for a fully generic approach, the second category of approach tried to decompose an image into layers of homogeneous information. The most recent and advanced work used Mathematical Decomposition or Morphological Component Analysis (MCA) [6,9]. MCA allows to separate features in an image which present different morphological aspects based on fast transform/reconstruction operators. Here again, our maps are mainly composed of black connected components on a noisy background, and a lot of overlapping text and graphics exits. Modelling each component in a generic way will impose to model all the different kind of details in all maps to finally obtained an over-fitted model, or to manually post-process images like in [3].

Finally, the last category relies on the use of connected components. A lot of work have been done using the connexity of pixels in the litterature and seems to better fit to the features of our maps. Techniques mainly use the properties of the connected components, like [1] which use the generation of connected components and the application of the Hough transform in order to group together components into logical character strings which may then be separated from the graphics. Some bounding boxes (BB) of the components can also be used, like in [23], and used to compute some statistics (size of BB) to separate them. Using some automatic classification process, computed dynamically from the histogram for instance, the large graphical components can be discarded and the smaller graphics and text components kept.

Another work, based on such statistics, proposed to filter the components by their density [12]. Using this information, components were filtered to remove dashed lines. However, to properly filter out connceted components is not an easy task.

As presented before, the maps are composed of dark connected components on a light background (initially white but degraded by time and manipulations). Using connected components then appear as a natural choice where filtering the connected components is a difficult process. A recent subfield of mathematical morphology based on trees of connected components offers some strategies to decompose an image in layers of information [14,26]. This paper will propose to study this last solution.

The using of trees of connected components to separate in uniform layers of information, ancient documents which the layers have been "flattened" at printing, is an original approach. This has never been used for this type of application. Moreover, even if this method use some filters and the thresholds inside the filters are (for the moment) set up manually, they are the only parameters. So, this method is generic and allows to extract components with an intelligent binarization and especially not a global one.

3   Tree of Connected Components

Mathematical morphology based on trees of connected components offers some strategies for obtaining meaningful hierarchical partitions from any hierarchical representation of an image. Classical connected components filtering techniques can be seen as shape-space filtering. Here, our idea is to apply some morphological operators to the shape graph-space of connected components extracted from the image. Then working on a tree rather than directly on the image will be much more efficient as maps are quite large (resolution of 9808×11824 pixels). The proposed method is based on the construction of a tree of all connected components of the input image. Then, on this tree, the components that do not correspond to the expected layers will be filtered out using their intrinsic properties.

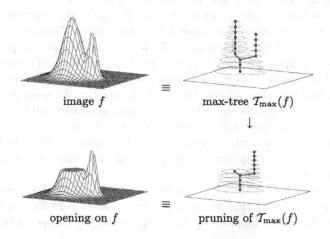

image f ≡   max-tree $\mathcal{T}_{\max}(f)$

opening on f ≡   pruning of $\mathcal{T}_{\max}(f)$

Fig. 2. A morphological connected operator (here an opening) based on a tree-based representation.

3.1   Definition

Whereas the most popular operators of mathematical morphology (MM) relies on structuring elements, the class of "connected operators" does not [14,21]. This class is very interesting because it satisfies the same numerous properties (and invariances) of MM operators, but with an additional property: connected operators do not shift object contours (they cannot create some new contours, they just suppress some existing ones). Formally, φ is a *connected operator* if, applied on any image f, we have:

$$\forall x \mathcal{N} x', \quad \varphi(f)(x) \neq \varphi(f)(x') \Rightarrow f(x) \neq f(x'),$$

where $\mathcal{N}$ is a neighborhood relationship. Some connected operators can be easily defined from some tree-based representations of a grey-level image [13,19,20]; such image representations express the inclusion of the connected components obtained by thresholding the image. Note that computing, storing, and processing such a component tree is very efficient [4,16]. In the following, we focus on a particular tree, namely the *max-tree*, that leads to morphological *algebraic openings*, that are, operators γ which are: increasing $(f_1 \leq f_2 \Rightarrow \gamma(f_1) \leq \gamma(f_2))$, idempotent $(\gamma \circ \gamma = \gamma)$, and anti-extensive $(\gamma \leq \mathrm{id})$. Replacing the *max-tree* by the *min-tree* leads to morphological *algebraic closings*, ϕ, which are increasing, idempotent, and extensive $(\phi \geq \mathrm{id})$. In addition, openings and closings have a strong property, shared by many morphological operators; they are invariant by contrast changes ($\forall g$ non-decreasing, $\gamma \circ g = g \circ \gamma$; the same goes for ϕ). This particular property is of prime importance because it implies that such operators have the ability to filter low-contrasted objects in the same way as they do with high-contrasted ones.

The *upper threshold set* (also called *upper level set*) at a given grey-level λ of a grey-level image f defined on a domain Ω is the set:

$$[f \geq \lambda] = \{x \in \Omega; f(x) \geq \lambda\} \in \mathcal{P}(\Omega),$$

and, from the family of sets $\{[f \geq \lambda]\}_\lambda$ we can easily reconstruct f, using: $\forall x, f(x) = \arg\max_\lambda \{\lambda; x \in [f \geq \lambda]\}$. When we consider the inclusion relationship, the set of connected components (obtained with the operator $\mathcal{CC}$) of all the threshold sets of f can be arranged into a tree, called max-tree of f:

$$\mathcal{T}_{\max}(f) = \{\Gamma \in \mathcal{CC}([f \geq \lambda])\}_\lambda.$$

Such a tree is displayed in Fig. 2 (top right). If we prune this tree, such as in Fig. 2 (bottom right), we can reconstruct the function depicted in Fig. 2 (bottom left). Doing so, we have a way to construct an algebraic opening γ_α. This process can be defined thanks to a selector operator:

$$\mathrm{sel}_\alpha(\Gamma) = \begin{cases} \Gamma & \text{if } \alpha(\Gamma) \text{ is true,} \\ \emptyset & \text{otherwise,} \end{cases}$$

with the following constraint on α to ensure that it is a pruning: $\Gamma_1 \subset \Gamma_2 \Rightarrow \mathrm{sel}_\alpha(\Gamma_1) \subset \mathrm{sel}_\alpha(\Gamma_2)$. It is easy to see that we can use for α the comparison between an increasing attribute computed on a component and a threshold. For instance, with: $\alpha(\Gamma) = (\mathrm{card}(\Gamma) \leq N)$ we filter out any component of the max-tree which size (area, i.e., number of pixels) is below the threshold N, which leads to an *area opening* [24]. Pruning the same way the min-tree leads to an *area closing*.

Last, note that a larger class of filtering operators on trees have been defined in [27], and that there is a third morphological tree defined on threshold sets, called the *tree of shapes* [5,7,11].

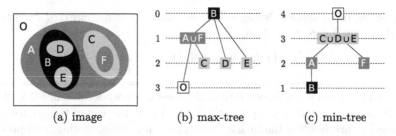

(a) image   (b) max-tree   (c) min-tree

Fig. 3. The dual morphological trees of the same image; light (resp. dark) grey values represent high (resp. low) integer values.

3.2 Building a Tree

The connected component trees are used to select or prune parts of the images in an efficient manner. The max-tree (Fig. 3b) is a tree where grey values are ranked from the darkest to the lightest, and the min-tree (Fig. 3c) is the dual of the max-tree, as it ranks the grey values from the lightest to the darkest. A component tree can be computed directly on the original grey-scale image or, to be more robust to defects, to the result of some filtering process (for instance, some thin objects can be re-connected beforehand, so that the components of threshold sets are better formed).

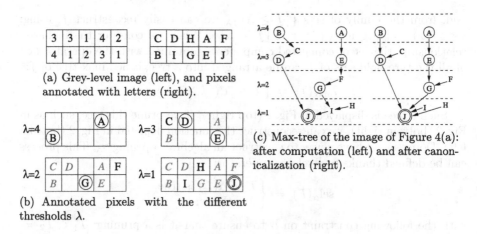

(a) Grey-level image (left), and pixels annotated with letters (right).

(b) Annotated pixels with the different thresholds λ.

(c) Max-tree of the image of Figure 4(a): after computation (left) and after canonicalization (right).

Fig. 4. Illustration of a max-tree computation.

To better understand how a component tree is built, we use a simple example to illustrate the process. Let us consider an image of 5×2 pixels having grey levels in the range $[1, 4]$ and, to make the explanations easier, let us name each pixel of the image by a letter going from A to J (see Fig. 4(a)).

For each pixel having a grey level $\lambda \geq 4$, two distinct connected components are obtained, which are {A} and {B}. Note that their surrounding pixels belong

```
FIND-ROOT(x)
1   if zpar(x) = x then return x
2     else { zpar(x) ← FIND-ROOT(zpar(x)) ; return zpar(x) }

COMPUTE-TREE(f)
1   for each p, zpar(p) ← undef
2   R ← REVERSE-SORT(f)    // maps R into an array
3   for each p ∈ R in direct order
4     parent(p) ← p ; zpar(p) ← p
5     for each n ∈ N(p) such as zpar(n) ≠ undef
6       r ← FIND-ROOT(n)
7       if r ≠ p then { parent(r) ← p ; zpar(r) ← p }
8   DEALLOCATE(zpar)
9   return pair(R, parent)    // a ''parent'' function

CANONICALIZE-TREE(parent, f)
1   for each p ∈ R in reverse order
2     q ← parent(p)
3     if f(parent(q)) = f(q) then parent(p) ← parent(q)
4   return parent    // a ''canonical'' parent function
```

Fig. 5. Code of the algorithm for creating a component tree.

to some other connected components. We then obtain two connected components, which are $\{A\}$ and $\{B\}$. In the next step, we move to the lower grey level value, here 3. We keep all pixels with a grey level value greater than or equal to 3. For each pixel having a grey level greater than or equal to 3, there are obtained two distinct connected components which are $\{A, E\}$ and $\{B, C, D\}$. Now we need to choose, for each connected component, a new pixel that is not part of the former connected components, and preferably the last pixel is taken in the reading direction of the image (Z-reading). In other words, the pixel D now represents the component $\{B, C, D\}$, obtained at threshold $\lambda = 3$, same thing with E for the component $\{A, E\}$. If we continue to apply the same approach for the rest of the image we obtain the results shown in Fig. 4(b). Finally the pixels of the image can be arranged into a rooted tree, shown in Fig. 4(c), where the arrows map a *parenthood* relationship.

In an equivalent manner, the min-tree of an image can be obtained going from the lowest to the highest grey level values.

The full algorithm, depicted in Fig. 5, takes only a few lines of code. There is nothing missing to be able to generate a tree of related components and is very easy to implement.

4   Extracting Map Components

4.1   Isolate Components

Based on the trees of connected components we have extracted, some components can be isolated by identifying their features. Note that the aim is to extract the content of the maps into several information layers, as shown in Fig. 1. So, we browse the created trees by filtering out the connected components that do not correspond to the required profile. Let us mention that computing some attributes related to connected components, and processing such trees to filter out or identify some particular connected components are very easy [25]. More details about these tree structures and their implementation are given in [4].

4.2   Strategy to Manage the Different Layers

As shown in Fig. 1 (right), fours layers have been extracted: French department names, borders, survey point numbers, and words in phonetics. To extract the different layers and to make the algorithm more robust, the following strategy has been adopted. When a layer has been extracted, the corresponding connected components are removed from the initial image in order to process the next layer. Indeed, ignoring already identified components helps to reduce errors while extracting new components. The French department names and survey point numbers have been extracted using this strategy. However, if something is misidentified in a given layer, it will be deleted for the next filtering. So the strategy consists in processing the easiest layers first. In this work, the choice has been to process the names of French departments (which are always surrounded by a rectangle), then the numbers of survey points (which are of fixed size), then the borders, and finally the words in phonetics (residue of the input image with the previous layers). The Fig. 6 shows the filtering system of the proposed method.

4.3   Extraction of French Department Names

Let us have a look at a concrete example on a map for filtering French department names. For this example, a whole scanned map of France has been chosen. The Fig. 7(a) shows a zoom of this map which is given in its entirety in input. Dark connected components on a light background need to be extracted.

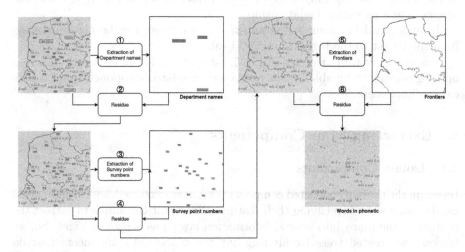

Fig. 6. The complete process of the filtering system for a map. Only a part of the map is shown, but the whole map was given for input and output.

For the French department names' extraction, the given input is the image of the map and there apply many filters to isolate French department names. A sampling of data allowed us to determine that these target objects were always surrounded by a rectangle, which vary in length but not in height. Rectangles are height invariant, but the length varies according to the name it contains. The minimum rectangle length that can be found on our example image is 130 pixels and the maximum is 433 pixels. The minimum rectangle height is 58 pixels and the maximum is 64 pixels, this is why we can consider that the height of the rectangles is invariant with regard to the height of the image (11824 pixels). With this informations, we considered that three types of filters should be implemented: a filter that recognize the vertical and horizontal lines of the picture to detect rectangles, a filter based on the dimensions of the components because rectangles are height invariant, and a filter based on the area of the components to filter the noise.

So the first step consists in isolating the vertical and horizontal lines from the rest. This strategy brings out all the rectangles of the map. Then a max-tree of new related components so formed will be created to try to fill in the rectangles that were highlighted in the previous step. On the min-tree created after the filling of the rectangles, a simple filter will be applied based on the properties of a connected component: if the white component at a height lower than the height of the rectangles we are trying to highlight, it is filled with the color of the parent component. So, all the small white components (the smallest components of the image being the inside of the rectangles) will be filled by a solid color (color of the outline of the rectangles), as shown in Fig. 7(b).

Since the expected properties of the components are known (height, width, area, etc.), another area filtering is applied to remove from the tree anything that does not correspond to what we expect. If the area of the component is smaller than the smallest rectangle, this component is deleted from the tree. This remove the noise that surrounds them (residues that match with very small rectangles).

Finally, we do the opposite filtering that filled the rectangles, using a min-tree instead of a max-tree, to remove the rectangles from the image and leave

(a) The map given in input.   (b) Image of the rectangle components of the map.   (c) Output image of the extraction of French department names.

Fig. 7. Different steps of French department names extraction (details).

only the outline of the map and the borders. The results, the isolation and extraction of French department names, lies in the residue of the two previous steps. We make the absolute difference of the image after removing the noise surrounding the rectangles with the image leaving only the outline of the map and the borders. The result of this filtering is shown in the Fig. 7(c).

4.4   Extraction of Survey Point Numbers

The filtering principle that was adopted for the French department names is adaptable to other information layers from the moment we know the properties of the connected components that we seek to extract. First of all, our goal is to bring out the desired connected components to the rest, and then we try to remove the noise that surrounds these connected components.

For the extraction of survey point numbers, the given input is the residue of the image of the map with the layer of French department names and there apply some area and dimension filtering to isolate survey point numbers. A sampling of data allowed us to determine that the survey point numbers objects were numbers ranging from 1 to 991 but discontinuously, and they are written in bold with always the same font. There is a maximum of 638 survey points on one map.

Survey point numbers are height invariant (font size), but the length varies according to the number it represents. The minimum survey point number length that can be found on our example image is 20 pixels and the maximum is 78 pixels. The minimum survey point number height is 36 pixels and the maximum is 45 pixels, this is why we can consider that the height of the survey point numbers is invariant with regard to the height of the image (11824 pixels). With this informations, we considered that two types of filters should be implemented: a filter based on the dimensions of the components because survey point numbers are height invariant, and a filter based on the area of the components to filter the noise. More, the mathematical morphology will be useful to group the numbers between them.

To extract this kind of components, the filtering consist to delete all the large components of the image. To isolate components, an area filter and a filter based on the size of the bounding boxes of the component are set up. If the property analyzed is above the defined thresholds (the largest area or dimension of a survey point number), the component take its parent's color in the min-tree (what will remove it from the image). The next step is to group numbers together (like chars to string), using mathematical morphology. This leads the last step of filtering, which is to remove the very small components (diacritics, frontiers made by dots, etc.) that remains on the image to get only the survey point numbers. To do this, as in the first filtering, an area filter and a filter based on the size of the bounding boxes of the component are set up. However this time, if the property analyzed is below the defined thresholds (the smallest area or dimension of a merged survey point number), the component take its parent's color in the min-tree (what will remove it from the image). The result of this step is an image containing only the survey point numbers, as shown in the right side of the Fig. 6.

4.5   Extraction of Frontiers and Phonetic Words

Three kind of frontiers can be find in the maps: solid lines (frontiers with the seas and oceans), dot-line-dot lines (border with bordering countries), and dot lines (border inside France). Two methods are used to extract this three kind of frontiers. The first one is really simple and based on the area of the connected components. In the atlas, the solid lines which correspond to the frontiers with the seas and oceans are always touching the outline of the map. It means that the area of this component is the bigger area that we can find in the image. So, you just have to look for the widest dark component of our tree, and you can extract this type of frontier pretty easily. The second method consists in extracting the dot lines and the dot-line-dot by the nearest neighbor search. This approach allows to draw a line between the dots to regroup them in only one set. This also has the advantage of eliminating all surrounding noise such as diacritics that could be assimilated to border points. To summarize, these two methods will make it possible to extract all the borders of the map in an automatic way. Once the borders have been identified and extracted from the map, it will remain, on the image given in input, only the words in phonetics (residue of the previous filtering steps).

5   Evaluation

In this section, we report performance indicators for the proposed approach. In this work, an open source image processing library was used to build the trees of connected components [15].

5.1   Protocol and Metric

We evaluated the task of detecting individual objects of the following types: names of French departments, and survey point numbers. The method under evaluation is presented with the original and complete image of a map, and produces a set of areas of interest, each of them being annotated with a type. Areas of interest are implemented as series of point coordinates forming polygons.

The evaluation is based on the metrics proposed in [22]: for each content type present in the ground truth and in the results for the method under test, we compute the following indicators:

"**correct**" (COR): the number of objects which were correctly detected, with the appropriate type (otherwise they are counted as noise for other content types);

"**missed**" (MIS): the number of objects which were expected in the ground truth for a particular content type, but were not detected by the method under test;

"noise" (NOI): the number of objects which were detected by the method under test but which do not correspond to any expected element in the ground truth.

A given ground truth element $g \in G$ is considered as correctly detected by a resulting element $d \in D$ if g and d verify the following relations, where T_a is an absolute threshold set to 0.5 and T_r is a relative threshold set to 0.2:

$$\frac{area(g \cap d)}{area(g)} > T_a \qquad \frac{area(g \cap d)}{\sum_{g' \in G, g' \neq g} area(g' \cap d)} > T_r$$

$$\frac{area(g \cap d)}{area(d)} > T_a \qquad \frac{area(g \cap d)}{\sum_{d' \in D, d' \neq d} area(g \cap d')} > T_r$$

For completeness, we also report in the results the **total number of expected objects** (NGT) of each type in the ground truth and the **total number of detected objects** (NDE), as well as the **precision** (PRE) and the **recall** (REC) for each content type. Those indicators have the following definitions:

$$NGT = COR + MIS \qquad NDE = COR + NOI$$

$$PRE = \frac{COR}{NDE} \qquad REC = \frac{COR}{NGT}$$

5.2　Data and Ground Truth

Annotated evaluation data was created from the original ALF map dataset. The dataset regroups 1950 maps. For each map, 3 types of information must be annotated: 84 names of departments, 638 survey point numbers, 638 words in phonetics. If all this had to be done by hand, it would take a long time. That is why we have decided to impose a few constraints on ourselves concerning the creation of the ground-truth. In the dataset, there are 7 types of maps (showing the different parts of France), that is why we decided to construct a ground-truth for each type of map to represent the atlas as much as possible while not spending too much time to do it. To save as much time as possible, we also decided to use the results of the current segmentation to avoid redoing everything from scratch and placing the points one by one, but to just move the points as precisely as possible if the segmentation is bad or missing.

One map showing France entirely was manually annotated to produce the ground truth for the task we previously introduced. This evaluation map (named "ALF0101" and visible in Fig. 7(a)) contains a total of 84 names of French departments, and 638 survey point numbers[3]. Each annotation is composed of a region described by a polygon and a content type described by a string: "French department", "survey", etc. Due to resource constraints, we could not annotate more maps. Our work is currently focused on the building of the ground-truth

---

[3] The ground truth of this evaluation map is available at http://l3i-share.univ-lr.fr/datasets/CarteALF0101.lif.

for the phonetics words on this map. After that, we will extend our ground-truth to other types of maps.

The dataset is composed by one atlas (ALF), which regroup 1950 maps. For each map, 3 types of information must be annotated: 84 names of departments, 638 survey point numbers, 638 words in phonetics. If all this had to be done by hand, it would take a long time. That is why we have decided to impose a few constraints on ourselves concerning the building of the ground-truth. In the dataset, there are 7 types of maps (showing the different parts of France), that is why we decided to construct a ground-truth for each type of map to represent the atlas as much as possible while not spending too much time doing it. To save as much time as possible, the results of the current segmentation will be used to avoid redoing everything from scratch and placing the points one by one, but to just move the points as precisely as possible if the segmentation is bad or missing.

5.3   Results

The results are presented in Table 1. Thanks to the trees of connected components and the filtering of the elements that compose them, the layer of information corresponding to the French department names can be successfully extracted. The position of French department names on the map can be easily determined. Concerning survey point numbers, the method was able to detect 86.36% for the target elements (551 items were well detected) while introducing 128 extra elements (noise).

Table 1. Results obtained on the map ALF0101.

	COR	MIS	NOI	NGT	NDE	PRE	REC
Names of French departments	84	0	0	84	84	100.0 %	100.0 %
Survey point numbers	551	87	128	638	679	81.2 %	86.4 %

The analysis of theses results show that some survey point numbers are missing ("MIS" column) because, in the original map, these components are directly connected to another bigger component, like frontiers. Survey point numbers are expected to be small components of the image, so large components (such as frontiers) are filtered at the beginning of the extraction step for this information layer, which also removes survey point numbers that touch those frontiers. The components wrongly detected as survey point numbers ("NOI" column) are all phonetic word letters that have not been well filtered during the extraction process because of their size similar to numbers.

6   Conclusion

In this paper, an extraction system for content of ancient maps using trees of connected components has been presented. The system take as input an image (scan of the map) and delivers different layers of information. Each layer correspond to a specific kind of information and there positions. The proposed approach uses a tree of connected components based on the grey level of the input image. Working on a tree rather than directly on the image will be much more efficient as maps are quite large. An adapted filtering of this tree allows to extract expected components by using their intrinsic properties. Thus, the method allows to localize the position of the extracted components.

The evaluation have given the number and the actual position of the components that are not correctly detected, the future works will consist on refining our approach in order to detect them more appropriately. Following the results, our approach needs to be modified to filter the numbers of survey points with a better accuracy. If this detection of survey point numbers is improved, this will allow us to perfectly detect phonetic words (residue of the basic image with all filtered layers) without missing or false-alarm components.

From the moment the layers of information are well identified, a system of text recognition in phonetics will be made. It should be based on an optical character recognition (OCR) method, and a dedicated recognition system that could be able to differentiate the many diacritics in phonetic words.

References

1. Fletcher, L.A., Kasturi, R.: A robust algorithm for text string separation from mixed text/graphics images. IEEE Trans. Pattern Anal. Mach. Intell. **10**(6), 910–918 (1988)
2. Bres, S., Eglin, V., Poulain, V.: Semi automatic color segmentation of document pages. CoRR, abs/1609.08393 (2016)
3. Cao, R., Tan, C.L.: Text/Graphics separation in maps. In: Blostein, D., Kwon, Y.-B. (eds.) GREC 2001. LNCS, vol. 2390, pp. 167–177. Springer, Heidelberg (2002). https://doi.org/10.1007/3-540-45868-9_14
4. Carlinet, E., Géraud, T.: A comparative review of component tree computation algorithms. IEEE Trans. Image Process. **23**(9), 3885–3895 (2014)
5. Carlinet, E., Géraud, T.: MToS: a tree of shapes for multivariate images. IEEE Trans. Image Process. **24**(12), 5330–5342 (2015)
6. Coustaty, M., Dubois, S., Ogier, J.-M., Menard, M.: Segmenting and indexing old documents using a letter extraction. In: Ogier, J.-M., Liu, W., Lladós, J. (eds.) GREC 2009. LNCS, vol. 6020, pp. 142–149. Springer, Heidelberg (2010). https://doi.org/10.1007/978-3-642-13728-0_13
7. Crozet, S., Géraud, T.: A first parallel algorithm to compute the morphological tree of shapes of nD images. In: Proceedings of the 21st IEEE International Conference on Image Processing (ICIP), Paris, France, pp. 2933–2937 (2014)
8. Dhar, D.B., Chanda, B.: Extraction and recognition of geographical features from paper maps. Int. J. Doc. Anal. **8**(4), 232–245 (2006)

9. Dubois, S., Péteri, R., Ménard, M.: Decomposition of dynamic textures using morphological component analysis. IEEE Trans. Circuits Syst. Video Techn. **22**(2), 188–201 (2012)

10. Ebi, N., Lauterbach, B., Anheier, W.: An image analysis system for automatic data acquisition from colored scanned maps. Mach. Vis. Appl. **7**, 148–164 (1994)

11. Géraud, T., Carlinet, E., Crozet, S., Najman, L.: A quasi-linear algorithm to compute the tree of shapes of nD images. In: Hendriks, C.L.L., Borgefors, G., Strand, R. (eds.) ISMM 2013. LNCS, vol. 7883, pp. 98–110. Springer, Heidelberg (2013). https://doi.org/10.1007/978-3-642-38294-9_9

12. Höhn, W.: Detecting arbitrarily oriented text labels in early maps. In: Sanches, J.M., Micó, L., Cardoso, J.S. (eds.) IbPRIA 2013. LNCS, vol. 7887, pp. 424–432. Springer, Heidelberg (2013). https://doi.org/10.1007/978-3-642-38628-2_50

13. Jones, R.: Component trees for image filtering and segmentation. In: Coyle, E. (ed.) Proceedings of the IEEE Workshop on Nonlinear Signal and Image Processing, Mackinac Island (1997)

14. Lazzara, G., Géraud, T., Levillain, R.: Planting, growing and pruning trees: Connected filters applied to document image analysis. In: Proceedings of the 11th IAPR International Workshop on Document Analysis Systems (DAS), IAPR, Tours, France, April 2014, pp. 36–40 (2014)

15. Lazzara, G., Levillain, R., Géraud, T., Jacquelet, Y., Marquegnies, J., Crépin-Leblond, A.: The SCRIBO module of the Olena platform: a free software framework for document image analysis. In: Proceedings of the 11th International Conference on Document Analysis and Recognition (ICDAR), IAPR, Beijing, China, September 2011, pp. 252–258 (2011)

16. Meijster, A., Wilkinson, M.H.F.: A comparison of algorithms for connected set openings and closings. IEEE Trans. Pattern Anal. Mach. Intell. **24**(4), 484–494 (2002)

17. Meyer, Y.: Oscillating Patterns in Image Processing and Nonlinear Evolution Equations. The Fifteenth Dean Jacqueline B. Lewis Memorial Lectures. American Mathematical Society, Boston (2001)

18. Rudin, L.I., Osher, S., Fatemi, E.: Nonlinear total variation based noise removal algorithms. Phys. D Nonlinear Phenom. **60**(1–4), 259–268 (1992)

19. Salembier, P., Oliveras, A., Garrido, L.: Antiextensive connected operators for image and sequence processing. IEEE Trans. Image Process. **7**(4), 555–570 (1998)

20. Salembier, P., Serra, J.: Flat zones filtering, connected operators and filters by reconstruction. IEEE Trans. Image Process. **3**(8), 1153–1160 (1995)

21. Salembier, P., Wilkinson, M.H.: Connected operators. IEEE Signal Process. Mag. **26**(6), 136–157 (2009)

22. Shafait, F., Keysers, D., Breuel, T.: Performance evaluation and benchmarking of six-page segmentation algorithms. IEEE Trans. Pattern Anal. Mach. Intell. **30**(6), 941–954 (2008)

23. Tombre, K., Tabbone, S., Pélissier, L., Lamiroy, B., Dosch, P.: Text/Graphics separation revisited. In: Lopresti, D., Hu, J., Kashi, R. (eds.) DAS 2002. LNCS, vol. 2423, pp. 200–211. Springer, Heidelberg (2002). https://doi.org/10.1007/3-540-45869-7_24

24. Vincent, L.: Grayscale area openings and closings, their efficient implementation and applications. In: Proceedings of the EURASIP 1st Workshop on Mathematical Morphology and its Applications to Signal Processing (ISMM), Barcelona, Spain, May 1993, pp. 22–27 (1993)

25. Xu, Y., Carlinet, E., Géraud, T., Najman, L.: Efficient computation of attributes and saliency maps on tree-based image representations. In: Benediktsson, J.A., Chanussot, J., Najman, L., Talbot, H. (eds.) ISMM 2015. LNCS, vol. 9082, pp. 693–704. Springer, Cham (2015). https://doi.org/10.1007/978-3-319-18720-4_58
26. Xu, Y., Carlinet, E., Géraud, T., Najman, L.: Hierarchical segmentation using tree-based shape spaces. IEEE Trans. Pattern Anal. Mach. Intell. **39**(3), 457–469 (2017)
27. Xu, Y., Géraud, T., Najman, L.: Connected filtering on tree-based shape-spaces. IEEE Trans. Pattern Anal. Mach. Intell. **38**(6), 1126–1140 (2016)

Extracting the February 1956 Ground Level Enhancement Event from Legacy Cosmic Ray Recordings

V. W. F. Mattana[1], G. R. Drevin[1(✉)], and R. D. Stauss[2]

[1] School of Computer Science and Information Systems, North-West University, Potchefstroom, South Africa
vwfmattana@gmail.com, gunther.drevin@nwu.ac.za
[2] School of Physical and Chemical Sciences, North-West University, Potchefstroom, South Africa
dutoit.strauss@nwu.ac.za

Abstract. Early continuous recordings of cosmic rays, as measured with Carnegie Type C Ionization Chambers, were made on rolls of photographic paper. This paper describes the extraction of the ionization data of the February 1956 ground level enhancement (GLE) event from the ionization chamber recordings of three stations, viz.: Godhavn, Cheltenham, and Christchurch.

To verify the accuracy of the extraction algorithm a ground truth image of historic cosmic ray recordings was first constructed from the original image. A synthetic version of the ground truth image, which to some degree, reproduced the distortions and optical artefacts present in the original image was then created from the ground truth image. The detection algorithm was then applied to the synthetic image and the extracted values compared to the ground truth image to evaluate the detection capabilities of the algorithm, using measures such as MSE, precision, accuracy and recall

The ionization data of the February 1956 GLE event was then extracted from the ionization chamber recordings and converted to percentage increase above background cosmic ray levels, for comparison to existing neutron monitor data which was sourced from a GLE database. The images share common attributes, and these include a sharp rise to a peak that tapers off more slowly. This trend is seen in all three data sets, and can be considered to be consistent with the neutron monitor data.

1 Introduction

The Carnegie Type C Ionization Chambers [1] or Model-C recorders were designed and built for the purpose of the continuous recording of cosmic rays. Essentially the ionization chamber was a steel sphere containing purified argon at a pressure of 50 atmospheres. The argon was ionized as cosmic rays passed through the chamber. A Lindemann electrometer was used to measure the ionization current.

© Springer Nature Switzerland AG 2018
A. Fornés and B. Lamiroy (Eds.): GREC 2017, LNCS 11009, pp. 131–143, 2018.
https://doi.org/10.1007/978-3-030-02284-6_10

To record the ionization level due to cosmic rays passing through the chamber, the shadow of the electrometer needle was projected onto a continuously moving strip of photographic paper. Furthermore, the barometric pressure and the temperature of the cosmic-ray meter could also be recorded on the same strip of photographic paper. Every hour the ionization chamber was grounded for 3 min, zeroing the ionization current and therefore bringing the electrometer needle back to the zero position. At the same time the lamp of the recorder was dimmed resulting in hourly vertical lines. Example recordings are shown in Fig. 1.

The sunspot records show that there was a steady increase in solar activity during the first half of the 20th century. It is only during the second half of the 20th century that neutron monitors and satellites have been used to monitor cosmic rays. Monitoring of cosmic rays using these more sophisticated methods have therefore been restricted to an era of high solar activity. Our knowledge of the sun indicates that it will return to low activity levels sometime in the future with serious implications for our modern technological infrastructure as well as for space travel. The only available source of continuous cosmic ray data for a period of increasing solar activity is the recordings made by the Carnegie Type C Ionization Chambers. This data is therefore of vital importance in studies of the manner in which cosmic rays respond to changes in the level of solar activity.

Ground level enhancements (GLEs) are sudden increases in the intensity of cosmic rays. This increase is caused by accelerated charged articles from the sun due to energetic eruptions on the sun. The two events of March 1942 are the first to be recorded. On average there has been one such an event per year since then.

The aim of this study is to test algorithms for the extraction of cosmic ray data on the GLE event of February 1956 for which comparable scientifically approved data is available. The creation of a synthetic ground truth image is a secondary aim, which is required to fulfill the primary aim of the study. This study is part of a larger study to extract and recover over 25 years of historic cosmic ray data recorded from 1935 until 1960. This study is an extension of the work done by [3,4,6].

The GLE event which occurred in February 1956 (GLE #5) was recorded by the Model-C recorder and these recordings have been digitised. A digital image processing algorithm was created to automatically extract the data contained in each scan of the photographic paper originally used to record the cosmic ray data. The extracted data will be compared with existing data for GLE #5, to test the feasibility of recovering as much of the cosmic ray data as possible. This data can be used in both long term space weather research, with the focus on weekly and monthly averages, as well as solar activity research, which is more focused on high resolution event data.

2   Data Used

The images used in this study document GLE #5, which occurred at about 4:30am UTC, from stations located at:

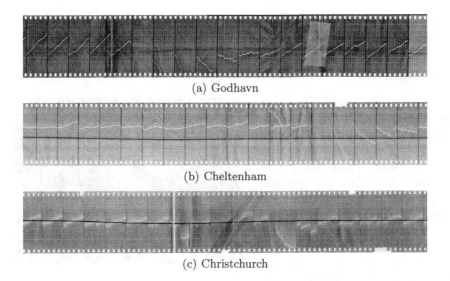

(a) Godhavn

(b) Cheltenham

(c) Christchurch

Fig. 1. GLE #5 on 23/2/1956 was recorded by the Model-C recorders at Godhavn (Greenland), Cheltenham (USA) and Christchurch (New Zealand). The white irregular line is the ionization current and the thick horizontal black line is the barometric pressure. There is no temperature trace on these recordings. The horizontal white lines are scale lines while the vertical black lines are hour markers.

1. Godhavn, Greenland: 69.2° North and 53.5° West. 9 m above sea level.
2. Cheltenham, U.S.A: 83.7° North and 76.8° West. 72 m above sea level.
3. Christchurch, New Zealand: 43.5° South and 172.6° East. 8 m above sea level.

The images measure approximately 6000 by 905 pixels, have a pixel depth of 24 bits and document a 19 h period (Fig. 1). To date more than 19000 such images have been scanned from the complete set of recordings.

The white irregular line in Fig. 1 is the ionization current and the thick horizontal black line is the barometric pressure. The horizontal white lines are scale lines while the vertical black lines are hour markers.

The section that is used documents the period from 2:30am–6:30am on 23/02/1956 (Fig. 2). This section was chosen as it details GLE #5 during its peak activity, and showcases some of the most challenging aspects of the historical data. Some of the data lines exceed the limits of the photographic paper; there is damage to the paper in the form of folds and creases in the film. There are also notations, such as the time and the date. Noticeably, the time is marked as '4'. There is also damage to one of the top perforations, and an hour marker is damaged.

3   Image Processing

This section deals with the image processing steps in the algorithm, and will be described below. The image processing is undertaken with a specific goal at each step such as to detect and locate a specific feature, viz. sprockets, hour markers, scale lines, or ionization data lines.

3.1 Sprockets

One can safely assume that the most prominent artefact in the input image would be the holes punched in the paper, known as the sprockets. These holes were punched into the photographic paper by the manufacturers, as these holes were necessary to drive the photographic paper. In this step the aim is to find and remove the sprockets from the input image. The sprockets produce areas of high intensity during to the scanning process. These bright spots disrupt the histogram,

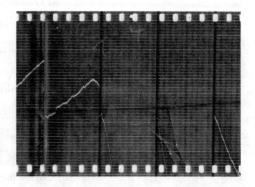

Fig. 2.   2:30am–6:30am   on   23/02/1956, recorded at Godhavn.

and make accurate binarization very difficult. These sprockets must be located and removed from our working image if any progress is to be made in extracting the other features. Firstly, a good sample perforation must be located on the image. Then the rest of the sprockets can be found automatically, making the process more user friendly. This is accomplished by finding the maximum of the correlation function between an ideal perforation profile, and the input RGB image. The pixels of the sprockets found in this way are then set to Not a Number (NaN). This results in the sprockets being removed from our image, which is now ready for further pre-processing.

3.2 Pre-processing

Once the sprockets have been removed the input image is ready to be converted to gray scale This step is focused on converting the colour image into a gray scale image with good contrast. Due to the size of the image, and the variance of intensity across the image, a block processing procedure is implemented. The block size is set at 20×20 pixels, to ensure that no attribute occupies the entire block at once. The resulting gray scale image is then histogram equalized. This histogram-equalised gray scale image is now ready to undergo binarization, separating the foreground from the background.

A user edited image can also be supplied to the algorithm, to assist in detecting areas of ambiguity. These areas include problems such as hour markers which are the "wrong" colour, data lines which are too faint to accurately extract, or unexpected holes in the paper which complicate thresholding.

3.3 Binarization

The binarization step of the image processing procedure is focused on creating a low noise binary image, with the attributes of the recording in white, and the background in black. Many different techniques for document image binarization have been proposed, and could be used to binarize the historic cosmic ray recordings, but the work of Sauvola and Pietikainen [8] and the improvements made thereupon by Gatos *et al.* [5] were the most effective in our application. Otsu's method [7] was also used to isolate the hour markers. These techniques have all the necessary methods we need for the binarization of the historic cosmic ray recordings. The process of binarization was approached by making use of a blockwise process (block size of 20 × 20 pixels), to negate the effect of varying background intensity over the image. This blockwise procedure used an iterative process to determine the best threshold. A starting threshold was found using Otsu's [7] method, and applied to the block. The total number of foreground pixels in the binarized block was counted, and this value was used as a measure of the block's brightness, referred to as the percentage of 'ON' pixels in a block. The threshold obtained from Otsu's method is then modified depending on the count of 'ON' pixels in the block. Calculations by the author show that the foreground elements occupy roughly 20% in an average block, and as such the 'ON' pixel percentage should be similar.

Consider a hour segment 900 pixels in height, and 300 pixels in length; the hour marker is 15 pixels wide on average, and as such occupies 5% of the vertical space in the image. There are on average 60 scale lines per hour marker segment, each about 2 pixels thick. These scale lines occupy at most 14% of the image. The data lines are less easily defined, but can be estimated to occupy about 2% of the image, due to overlap with the already counted scale lines and hour markers. The thickness of the data lines will vary from hour segment to hour segment, as well as between different recordings. As such the ideal value of 'ON' pixel percentage in an hour marker segment lies between 19% and 21% 'ON' pixels per segment. The segments are not ideal however and this threshold is broadened to 16–22% depending on the image being investigated.

The threshold is adjusted up or down to move the 'ON' percentage closer to the calculated values. This process is iterated until the 'ON' percentage is between 16% and 22%, with the upper bound being slightly tighter, to reduce the effect of noise in the background.

At this stage it is useful to note the *width* of a line, as referred to later in the text, is measured perpendicular to the line in question. For example, the width of a scale line (horizontal) is the vertical dimension of the scale line, whereas the width of a vertical line such as an hour marker is its horizontal dimension.

3.4 Hour Markers

The next step is to locate the hour markers, or vertical black lines, using the results of the previous steps to assist this process. The gray scale image is divided into 20 segments, each spanning the height of the image. For each segment, the column totals are determined, and a moving average is found (5 pixels wide) for each column. The column with the lowest moving average is selected as a candidate hour marker, and is transcribed onto the blank output image. In this way, we find up to 21 potential hour markers, even though only 19 of them will be true hour markers, due to the first or last one being cut off at some length. Once the entire image has been processed as described, and the candidate hour markers have been found, the false hour markers are removed, using the a-priori knowledge (the average separation of the hour markers for the current image). Any hour markers within less than 285–310 pixels of the previous hour marker will be removed (depends on recording station, as an average separation for the hour markers is determined as the algorithm proceeds through the image).

Once the hour markers have been located it is possible to segment the image according to the hour markers. This segmentation is first used to determine the angle at which the hour marker lies, cropping a window 31 pixels wide around each hour marker location. The angle of the hour marker is found by using the Hough transform of the edges of this line. From the resulting lines, the most prominent line is drawn onto a blank image. Once the angle, θ, has been found using the Hough transform, a new hour marker must be drawn in at this angle, however, the hour marker's pivot point is not at the top of the image, but rather near the middle of the image's height. From Eq. 1, one is able to find the horizontal distance, $2d$, of a line drawn from the top of

Fig. 3. Diagram of the inherent skew of the hour markers.

the image, to the bottom, at an angle θ (Fig. 3). Once this distance is known, the new hour marker can be drawn with the pivot position in the centre of the image's height using half this distance, d.

$$d = \frac{tan(\theta) * H}{2}. \tag{1}$$

This new hour marker is then used as a mask, and shifted left and right, until a minimum intensity is found. At this stage the new tilted hour marker is drawn onto the final hour marker image. These tilted hour markers will be used as the ground truth hour markers from this point forward.

3.5   Scale Lines

After the hour markers have been found, the histogram equalized gray scale image is segmented along the middle of each hour marker line. This step's aim is to locate scale lines, in each segment, as accurately as possible. In this way each hour segment is inspected individually and the continuous scale lines and data lines can be located. Due to the varying intensity of the scale lines on the images, the decision was made to approach each hour marker segment as an individual set of scale lines. The scale line location process is also a block processing technique, using blocks that span the width of the image, and allow 60 such blocks to fit into the image. This ensures roughly 2 scale lines will be visible in each block. The row sums of the block are then obtained, and a running average of 3 pixels is determined for each row total. The maximum row in the block is marked on a black output image as a candidate scale line. Once all candidate scale lines have been marked, the output image is checked against a-priori knowledge, such as the average separation, width, and count. False scale lines are removed, and estimated scale lines are inserted where scale lines are missing. These candidate scale lines are then individually adjusted to lie on the local maxima of column intensity. These lines are then used as a guiding rail, for finding the real scale lines per column. This technique uses a candidate system spanning 5 pixels above and below each guide scale line, with the moving average of 3 pixels in width. This process gives us an accurate description of the local maxima along the scale line approximations, which reflect the scale lines.

3.6   Data Lines

This step is concerned with locating the ionization data line in each hour segment. As the scale lines are the brightest regions on the image, we can use this information to our advantage, by inspecting the regional maxima of the grey scale image. However, the scale lines will also be registered as regional maxima, and as such the scale lines need to be eliminated. Care must be taken in removing scale lines, as the scale lines overlap with the data. The solution is to subtract the average scale line intensity from a small neighbourhood around the scale lines that have been found previously. This way the brighter region of the scale line where the data line crossed remains bright, whereas the rest of the scale line is far less intense. The regional maxima of the grey scale image are then de-noised using morphological opening, with an structuring element of 25 pixels in size. The remaining region is a good description of the where the data can be found. This region is then used as a mask, and the column-wise candidate process is undertaken again, this time with a moving average of 5 pixels in size. This returns a data line for regions detected by the regional maxima algorithm provided by Matlab.

4   Ground Truth

The result of the image processing steps detailed in the previous section yields a ground truth image. This ground truth image represents the structures in the original images, specifically, the hour markers, scale lines, and ionization data line. The hour markers are 5 pixels wide, while the rest of the elements are a single pixel thick. Upon first inspection one will notice missing sections of scale lines. However, if one inspects Fig. 2 closely, it becomes apparent that there are sections where the dark pressure line has removed a scale line, or part thereof.

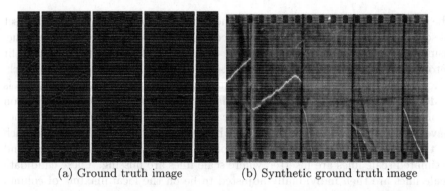

(a) Ground truth image　　　　(b) Synthetic ground truth image

Fig. 4. (a) Ground truth image, with hour markers (vertical), scale lines (horizontal), and ionization data (nonlinear line). (b) Synthetic ground truth image produced by the algorithm.

This ground truth image is built directly of measurable properties of the input image.

The ground truth image will be used in conjunction to a histogram equalized grayscale version of the original image to extract the ionization data. A sample of a ground truth image is shown in Fig. 4(a).

5　Synthetic Image

The ground truth images were used as a skeleton upon which in-painting [2] could be used to reconstruct the texture of the original image. As such, the intersect of the ground truth and the grayscale image was used as a seed for inpainting. The resulting synthetic image can be used to visually compare the results, as well as having potential uses in extraction algorithm optimization. The result is visually similar, with the benefit of not having sprockets with high intensity, (Fig. 4(b)). It is also based directly on the ground truth image, which can be of use when testing alternative data extraction techniques.

6　Ionization Data Lines

Arguably the most important feature on the recordings is the ionization data lines. These lines represent the ionization recorded by the Model-C recorder, and to obtain the percentage increase which GLE #5 produced, it is necessary to retrieve this attribute of the image as accurately as possible. The raw extracted data lines for the Godhavn observation of GLE #5 is shown in Fig. 5. The horizontal axis is marked with the pixel number on which the data point occurs, however this axis also represents time, with each pixel measuring approximately 12 s. The vertical axis is measured in pixel height. There are cases where no data points are located on a line, and as such the corresponding height value is stored as Not a Number (NaN). This extends to the discretized interval, and if there are no values in the interval, data will appear missing on Figs. 5, 6 and 7.

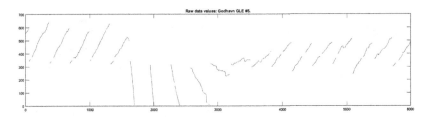

Fig. 5. The ionization data for the Godhavn image, with pixel height plotted against pixel location.

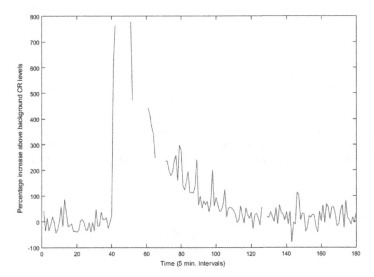

Fig. 6. Percentage increase above background cosmic ray levels at Godhavn 23/02/1956. A sharp increase and slower decrease are indicative of a GLE.

7 Accuracy of Extraction

The results of the analysis comparing the results of the test image to the original ground truth, for each of the three stations investigated (Table 1). The MSE row shows the mean square error between the extracted attributes and the ground truth image, as well as the MSE between the extracted ionization data line and the ground truth's data line. The MSE was calculated for each station using

$$MSE = \frac{1}{n}\sum_{i=1}^{n}(\hat{Y}_i - Y_i)^2 \tag{2}$$

and a lower value is better, as the error is lower. The MSE shows the total distance between pixels of the resulting data, and the pixels of the ground truth image.

When classifying the extracted pixels as true positives (tp), true negatives (tn), false positives (fp), and false negatives (fn), one can define precision, recall

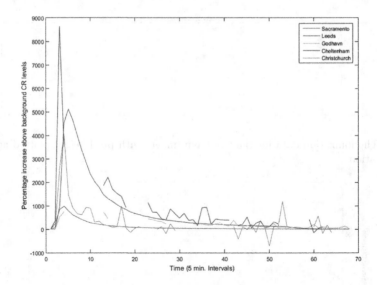

Fig. 7. A comparison of the ground truth data lines (Godhavn, Cheltenham, and Christchurch) to existing neutron monitor records (Leeds and Sacramento) [9]. The data begins at 3:50am UTC, with each interval representing 5 min, and ends at 9:45am.

and accuracy and recall as:

$$P = \frac{tp}{tp + fp} \tag{3}$$

$$R = \frac{tp}{tp + fn} \tag{4}$$

$$A = \frac{tp + tn}{tp + tn + fp + fn} \tag{5}$$

together with the F-measure were also calculated from the extracted attributes and the ground truth image, as well as the extracted ionization data line and the ground truth's data line. All of these measures are normalised to lie between 0–1, with a higher value being better.

8   Conversion

8.1   Ionization Data Binning

The raw location data was subjected to median binning, with each bin representing a five minute interval, and consisting of about 28 pixels (this number varies depending on the width of the hour section). The median was used instead of the average, due to the median's resistance to outliers and noise. The data sourced from the GLE database is recorded in 5 min intervals, and as such the decision was made to use 5 min intervals so as to match the existing data. This

Table 1. Precision of results

Measure	Godhavn		Cheltenham		Christchurch	
	Extract	Data	Extract	Data	Extract	Data
MSE	599.71	1.82	345.76	20.39	1446.9	34.36
Precision	0.9446	0.9822	0.9630	0.8108	0.8758	0.6222
Recall	0.9604	0.9868	0.9824	0.8291	0.8967	0.4813
Accuracy	0.9908	1.0000	0.9947	0.9997	0.9777	0.9995
F-Measure	0.9524	0.9845	0.9726	0.8199	0.8861	0.5428

will greatly simplify the comparison of the percentage increase data. As each individual Model-C recorder was calibrated separately, the constant needed to correct the data for these settings is specific to each recorder. This resulted in each machine having a different scaling constant, which means that the separation of the scale lines have different values attributed to them, based on the recording station's calibration constant. However, the gradient of the data line is where our percentage increase data can be found, using

$$Increase = \left([1 - \frac{I}{I_0}] \right) \times 100\%. \qquad (6)$$

where I represents the current segment's gradient, and is defined as:

$$I = \frac{\Delta c}{\Delta t}, \qquad (7)$$

with Δc being the change in the ionization level over a period of time Δt. The background cosmic ray level is given by I_0,

$$I_0 = \frac{\Delta c_0}{\Delta t}, \qquad (8)$$

with Δc_0 being the change in the background ionization level over a period of time Δt. Thus in this study we will only be considering the relative intensity/relative increase above background levels.

8.2 Percentage Increase

The gradient between each bin, or step in the data is of great interest. Using 6, the percentage increase over the bin length (five minutes) can be found. Figure 6 shows the percentage increase in the cosmic ray intensity over the background level for the full span of the image recorded at Godhavn. The missing segments are due to the data line reaching the bottom edge of the photographic paper before the Model-C recorder could reset its position the following hour.

9   Comparison

There are documented results from neutron monitors available for GLE #5, and these will be the values we will be comparing our results to. Due to the nature of the data, and calibration constants which are unknown at the time of writing this paper (due to fragmented log books), the shape of the percentage increase plot is the main feature we are interested in, as the height of the peak can be adjusted by using the correct constant for the particular machine which recorded the data. There is potentially a way to calibrate the data using temperature and pressure, but that is outside the scope of this study.

The percentage increase data which is used to compare GLE data is compared to that of neutron monitors from Leeds and Sacramento, as these locations offer insight into the range of GLE #5. The Leeds station is one of the stations with the smallest recorded percentage increase for GLE #5, whereas Sacramento has one of the highest recorded peaks for GLE #5. The extracted percentage increase above the background level is compared to the neutron monitor data from the GLE database for Leeds and Sacramento as comparative data sources, spanning the range of GLE #5 (Fig. 7). The important aspect of these graphs is their general shape, as the calibrations of the Model-C recorder are unknown to the author. Normalization constant should be applied to these curves, based on the pressure and temperature of the time and place where the recordings were taken. Additionally, parts of the data set are missing due to the limitations of the Model-C recorder.

The images do share common attributes, and these include a sharp rise to a peak which tapers off more slowly. This trend is seen in all three data sets, and can be considered to be consistent with the existing (more accurate) neutron monitor data. Additional discrepancies may be attributed to the inaccuracies of the Model-C recorder itself.

10   Conclusion and Future Work

In conclusion, GLE #5 has been extracted from historical GLE records with an acceptable level of accuracy, using automated image processing techniques. This study serves as a proof of concept, and validates ground truth images for further extraction of historical cosmic ray records. The synthetic image and ground truth, allow this algorithm to be used to test other extraction algorithms against.

Future work includes topics such as; long-term data extraction (daily, monthly, annual values), statistical rationale for binning decisions, user interface for user input, development and testing of better extraction algorithms, extraction of temperature and barometric pressure, normalization of the ionization data taking into account temperature and pressure and finding the correct calibration constants for the Model-C recorders used.

References

1. Compton, A., Wollan, E., Bennett, R.: A precision recording cosmic-ray meter. Rev. Sci. Instrum. **5**, 415–422 (1934)
2. D'Errico, J.: "Inpaint nans" matlab central file exchange (2012). https://www.mathworks.com/matlabcentral/fileexchange/4551-inpaint-nans/. Accessed 06 Oct 2016
3. Drevin, G.: Adaptive frequency domain filtering of legacy cosmic ray recordings. In: Proceedings of the 11th Joint Conference on Information Sciences, pp. 15–20 (2008)
4. Du Plessis, T.: Die versyfering van historiese kosmiese straal-data. M.Sc. thesis from the Potchefstroom Campus of the North-West University (2010)
5. Gatos, B., Praktikakis, I., Perantonis, S.: Adaptive degraded document image binarization. Pattern Recognit. **39**, 317–327 (2006)
6. Mattana, V., Drevin, G., Roux, P.: The creation of synthetic digital ground-truth images of historic cosmic ray data recordings. In: Lamiroy, B., Dueire Lins, R. (eds.) GREC 2015. LNCS, vol. 9657, pp. 19–30. Springer, Cham (2017). https://doi.org/10.1007/978-3-319-52159-6_2
7. Otsu, N.: A thresholding selection method from gray-level histograms. Automatica **11**(285–296), 23–27 (1975)
8. Sauvola, J., Pietikäinen, M.: Adaptive document image binarization. Pattern Recognit. **33**, 225–236 (2000)
9. Usoskin, I.: GLE database (2016). https://gle.oulu.fi. Accessed 25 Sep 2016

Reports and Summaries of the Discussion Groups

Engineering Drawing Challenge II

Bart Lamiroy[1(✉)] and Daniel P. Lopresti[2]

[1] Université de Lorraine – Loria (UMR 7503), Campus scientifique,
BP 239, 54506 Vandœuvre-lès-Nancy Cedex, France
`Bart.Lamiroy@loria.fr`
[2] Department of Computer Science and Engineering, Lehigh University,
113 Research Drive, Bethlehem, PA 18015, USA

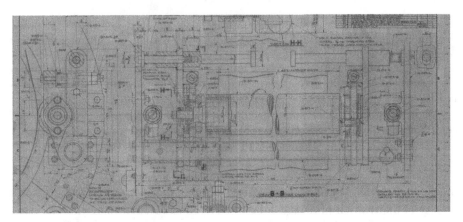

Abstract. The first GREC Engineering Drawing Challenge (http://
iapr-tc10.univ-lr.fr/index.php/conferences/contest?id=297) was held in
2015. Since then, more than 800 high definition engineering drawings
have been digitized and made available to the research community,
accounting for approximately 400 GB of unique image data. The collection is available on the Lehigh University DAE server (http://dae.cse.
lehigh.edu/DAE/?q=browse/dataitem/606796).

The 2015 edition gave rise to a number of challenges and ideas specifically targeted to Graphics Recognition and were published in the proceedings of the GREC workshop. They are still relevant and open questions, and need to be addressed by the research community.

This year, we are launching a complementary and different challenge...

1 Introduction

In 2011, hundreds of engineering drawings have been made available to the
Graphics Recognition research community thanks to joint efforts between Lehigh
University and the IAPR TC-10. This collection has been called the "Lehigh
Steel Collection" [1]. It is comprised of both hand- and computer-made drawings
during the 1960's to the 1990's. Subsequent efforts by various research groups
has contributed to curating and digitizing part of these documents in order to

© Springer Nature Switzerland AG 2018
A. Fornés and B. Lamiroy (Eds.): GREC 2017, LNCS 11009, pp. 147–151, 2018.
https://doi.org/10.1007/978-3-030-02284-6_11

make them available for document image analysis research purposes. This process is still ongoing. The collection is available on the Lehigh University DAE server (http://dae.cse.lehigh.edu/DAE/?q=browse/dataitem/606796) [4]. Furthermore, a first initiative has been launched in order to provide an inventory of challenges this data collection can help solve [3]. The new challenge, presented here, results from observed artefacts in the collection, due to the digitization process.

2   Transforming (partial) Failure into Opportunity

After the process of digitizing the 800 engineering drawings was finished, a quality inspection of the data has shown artifacts induced by the scanning process. These artifacts most definitely come from flaws in the digitization apparatus and may be combination of hardware failures and firmware compensation errors. They consist of colored, perfectly vertical, narrow stripes in the image, as shown in Fig. 1.

Digitization was done on a ColorTrack smartLF Gx+42 (https://www.colortrac.com/scanner/smartlf-gx-42/) at 400dpi by Ingecap (http://ingecap.fr/). Images are full color lossless TIFF and approximately 15000 × 9000 pixels large for 400MB each. They can be downloaded for inspection[1].

On the one side, the artifacts are of sufficient importance to produce significant bias in standard image analysis results. As such the resulting overall quality of digitization process can be considered as incompatible with the standards required for high quality reference research data (hence, the *"failure"*). On the other hand, a close inspection of the nature of the artifacts (their regularity, their repetitive frequency pattern, their non destructive nature . . .) and the volume of the available data (400 GB) most of which has a more than acceptable level of quality, makes is plausible that some well thought-out post-processing software may be able to filter out these artifacts, and an *opportunity* to conduct some exciting state-of-the-art benchmarking to see where our research community currently stands with respect to large real-world document image analysis (Is the problem at hand *"easy"* with respect to the current state-of-the-art? Is it *"interesting"* with respect to evaluating other document analysis challenges? Can current mechanisms effectively handle the quantity and size of data?).

3   Presentation and Preliminary Artifact Analysis

The ColorTrack (https://www.colortrac.com/scanner/smartlf-gx-42/) series are roller scanners with a fixed 1D array of CCDs under which the document is fed and progressively moved by a traction system. This is important to notice, since it allows to make some very strong assumptions about the artifacts. The artifacts

---

[1] http://dae.cse.lehigh.edu/DAE/?q=browse/dataitem/606796.

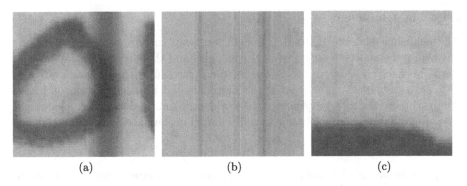

(a)   (b)   (c)

Fig. 1. From left to right: example of artifact crossing drawing, showing that the underlying signal is not entirely lost (a); artifacts appearing essentially in CYM thus hinting to a defect in one of the CCD channels (b) ; example of more subtle, evanescent artifacts (c).

are depicted in Fig. 1 (high resolution versions of these images are available[2]). Their intensity may be varying from extremely weak and barely visible to very strong.

We have identified 3 types of artifacts that may probably require different approaches as to their handling and filtering. We presume that their difficulty in handling is probably increasing with the order of presentation below.

1. Strong full length artifacts, as shown in Fig. 1a. They are highly saturated in one of the CYM channels, and by design of the scanner are perfectly vertical lines, running all over the scanned document.
2. Soft full length artifacts, as shown in Fig. 1b. They are not as saturated, nor as high intensity as the previous ones. Still they seem to be essentially composed of one of the CYM channels, and still are perfectly vertical lines, running all over the scanned document.
3. Partial length artifacts, as shown in Fig. 1c. They seem not to be running over the whole page, and of varying, often very weak intensity.

Because of their supposed origin (hardware or firmware defect on some of the CCD sensors) all artifacts share the properties of being perfectly vertical. Each stripe is consistent in color, although there seems to be no obvious color consistency between different stripes. The majority of artifacts cover the whole height of the image. A minority of artifacts seem to appear only on a part of given scan lines, and not covering the entire height. A sample image showing this at full resolution is available for download[3].

---

[2] http://grec2017.loria.fr/wp-content/uploads/2017/07/zoomsnap1.png,   http://grec2017.loria.fr/wp-content/uploads/2017/07/extreme.png, http://grec2017.loria.fr/wp-content/uploads/2017/07/Light-Stripes.png.

[3] http://dae.cse.lehigh.edu/DOWNLOADS/example.tif.

3.1   The Challenge

The challenge consists in finding an efficient way to remove the artifacts by leveraging the specific context of both the data, and the structural properties of the noise itself. This seems to be an unique opportunity to combine and compare state-of-the-art knowledge of the Graphics and broader Document Image Analysis domains to a large scale real-world problem, and to create the conditions for collaboration, exchange and discussion on large scale document image processing.

Requirements and Contributions. In order to compete and contribute to the challenge contenders should provide:

- a *standalone software solution* (executable code, script or network service) that takes a single image as an input and provides a filtered image of the same dimensions and encoding as output and from which the artifacts are removed and replaced by a plausible set of pixels rendering the supposed original image.
- a *full description* of the techniques and methods applied to achieve the filtering; this description should take the form of a publishable, or published paper.

The requirement of a standalone solution is merely a necessity for allowing to assess, compare and evaluate various contributions in a homogeneous and straightforward way, without any possible bias towards parameter tuning.

It should be obvious to the contenders that pretraining and fine-tuning parameters to fit the specific data set can be integrated in the proposed solutions.

Evaluation and Assessment. This challenge has the specific property of not having a predetermined formal *"Ground-Truth"* solution, nor has it the traditional training, testing and evaluation subsets. This is making the evaluation and assessment of contributions a challenge in itself.

For evaluation we will be combining two techniques: statistical metrics designed to compute performance evaluation without reference data, as published in [2,5], and crowd-sourced peer evaluation.

The latter will consist of random sampling relevant image patches and submitting them to human evaluators (typically the contestants) for assessment under the following form: *"Given the original image patch, which one of two randomly selected contributed methods provides better results in removing the artifacts?"*. The compiled results over a reasonable, yet significant amount of patches combined with a Condorcet voting (https://en.wikipedia.org/wiki/Condorcet_method) tally will allow for ranking all contributing methods.

Tentative Timeline and Deadlines. Contestants can join and contribute at any time in the process. There is no clear and established timeline, nor deadline. The goal is to progressively and regularly report contributions and improvements.

Progress reports will be presented and made available on a regular basis at the usual IAPR (International Association for Pattern Recognition) events dedicated to Document Analys such as GREC (http://grec2017.loria.fr/), ICDAR (http://u-pat.org/ICDAR2017/) and DAS 2018 (https://das2018.caa.tuwien.ac.at/).

A dedicated website and related services for assessment and comparison of methods will be set up in due time. And a permanent contact address is available at eng-drawings-contest@loria.fr.

References

1. Bruno, B., Lopresti, D.P.: The lehigh steel collection: a new open dataset for document recognition research. In Coüasnon, B., Ringger, E.K. (eds.) Document Recognition and Retrieval XXI, San Francisco, California, USA, 5–6 February 2014. SPIE Proceedings, vol. 9021, pp. 90210O–90210O-9. SPIE (2014)
2. Fedorchuk, M., Lamiroy, B.: Statistic metrics for evaluation of binary classifiers without ground-truth. In: IEEE First Ukraine Conference on Electrical and Computer Engineering (UKRCON), Kiev, Ukraine. IEEE, May 2017
3. Lamiroy, B., Lopresti, D.P.: Challenges for the engineering drawing lehigh steel collection. In: Eleventh IAPR International Workshop on Graphics Recognition - GREC 2015, August 2015
4. Kerautret, B., Colom, M., Monasse, P. (eds.): RRPR 2016. LNCS, vol. 10214. Springer, Cham (2017). https://doi.org/10.1007/978-3-319-56414-2
5. Lamiroy, B., Sun, T.: Computing precision and recall with missing or uncertain ground truth. In: Kwon, Y.-B., Ogier, J.-M. (eds.) GREC 2011. LNCS, vol. 7423, pp. 149–162. Springer, Heidelberg (2013). https://doi.org/10.1007/978-3-642-36824-0_15

Discussion Group Summary: Optical Music Recognition

Jorge Calvo-Zaragoza[1(✉)], Jan Hajič Jr.[2], and Alexander Pacha[3]

[1] PRHLT Research Center, Universitat Politècnica de València, Valencia, Spain
jcalvo@prhlt.upv.es
[2] Institute of Formal and Applied Linguistics, Charles University,
Prague, Czech Republic
hajicj@ufal.mff.cuni.cz
[3] Institute of Visual Computing and Human-Centered Technology, Vienna, Austria
alexander.pacha@tuwien.ac.at

Abstract. This document summarizes the discussion of the interest group on Optical Music Recognition (OMR) that took place in the 12th IAPR International Workshop on Graphics Recognition, and presents the main conclusions drawn during the session: OMR should revisit how it describes itself, and the OMR community should intensify its collaboration both internally and with other stakeholders.

Keywords: Optical Music Recognition · Discussion group

1 Introduction

The 12th IAPR International Workshop on Graphics Recognition (GREC'17) hosted an interest group on Optical Music Recognition (OMR), a field of research that is concerned with computationally reading music notation in documents. OMR has been an active research field for decades, but so far it is (justifiably) known to "not work", at least not well enough for real-world use-cases.

The workshop was a unique opportunity for the field to reflect its state, as representatives of most active OMR research groups were present, thanks to the numerous workshop contributions related to the subject (10 out of 27 contributions at GREC'17). The attendees of the meeting were (in alphabetical order): Jorge Calvo-Zaragoza, Kwon-Young Choi, Jan Hajič jr., Jose M. Iñesta, Alexander Pacha, Zeyad Saleh, and Ké Zhang; Alicia Fornés spent some time in the discussion group as well.

The discussion uncovered broader systemic issues that hinder the progress of OMR towards usable systems, rather than just a lack of technical solutions. In this paper, we present the two most salient points that OMR needs to address:

– Revisiting how OMR is defined and described. This is necessary to design OMR systems that address actual needs and to accurately communicate the state of the art (Sect. 2).

J. Calvo-Zaragoza et al.—Equal contribution.

© Springer Nature Switzerland AG 2018
A. Fornés and B. Lamiroy (Eds.): GREC 2017, LNCS 11009, pp. 152–157, 2018.
https://doi.org/10.1007/978-3-030-02284-6_12

– Intensifying collaboration within the OMR community and with related fields, and making contributions to OMR more interoperable (Sect. 3).

2   Redefining OMR

The discussion group uncovered critical gaps in how OMR talks about itself. There is some intuitive understanding of what OMR is, and the standard pipeline [1,9,19] has been a helpful scaffold for decomposing OMR systems into manageable steps, but the field is starting to outgrow these foundations. For instance, with respect to methods, the traditional staff-line removal step [6] is no longer required in some systems before detecting musical symbols [10,17], and there are even end-to-end OMR systems that do away with most intermediate steps [5,21].

More importantly, OMR has been with few exceptions implicitly treated as a monolithic problem, with the accompanying assumption that it has a single goal, or at least a theoretically ideal output representation that OMR systems should produce (which may then be used for various purposes). As became evident while discussing a possible future OMR competition, this is not the case: it turns out there is only limited consensus on what are worthwhile objectives to compete in.

Existing OMR literature is of little help in this respect. The overwhelming majority of publications naturally focus on methods used to "solve OMR" [16, 19]. Some works are devoted to evaluation [2,7,13,18], and a paper by Byrd and Simonsen [3] analyses the various dimensions of OMR difficulty. However, there is no systematic treatment of the theoretical underpinnings of OMR: What is it actually trying to achieve? What is the internal structure of the field? There is an established taxonomy of OMR systems according to the inputs they process, but what is the taxonomy of OMR systems according to the *outputs* they should produce? Without a clearer idea of what OMR is expected to achieve, it is difficult to correctly evaluate sub-system improvements in the context of eventual OMR applications, and to communicate these advances — and their limitations — to stakeholders who are waiting for systems to be ready for their use-cases. Furthermore, such an analysis would make the problem of evaluating OMR more manageable as well.

The natural conclusion to this point of GREC'17 discussion is that an analysis of the field from the perspective of its goals and outputs should be performed and published.

3   Collaboration and Interoperability

Optical Music Recognition is by virtue of its domain interdisciplinary. Its motivations come not only from musicians and composers, but also from music libraries, musicology (especially its digital branch), and music information retrieval. On the other hand, none of these fields has the tools to provide solutions. For these,

OMR practitioners need to look to image processing, specifically document processing and pattern/graphics recognition, machine learning, and, in recent years, deep learning.

This dichotomy between communities that appreciate OMR results and those that can provide constructive feedback on OMR methods leads to the situation where OMR-related publications get scattered, and consequently their authors rarely meet in person. In this respect, the assembly of OMR researchers at the GREC'17 workshop was rather unique and was only possible because of a concerted effort of a member of the Program Committee, who reached out to active OMR researchers individually (since the field is small, this is manageable).

The International Society for Music Information Retrieval (ISMIR) conference has recently started attracting OMR contributions more naturally, since deep learning methods have proliferated in the music information retrieval community to the extent that deep learning-based OMR is a natural fit for the conference both in terms of applications and methods. However, despite these developments, the OMR community remains loose and its outputs are rarely inter-operable so that in effect it is difficult to actually build upon previous work.

Open-source software has, fortunately, become the (academic) norm. One has, e.g., Audiveris[1], the Pixel.js [20] and MUSCIMarker [11] data annotation tools, the pre-trained symbol detection models of Pacha et al. [17] in the Diva.js framework, and the CVC-MUSCIMA [8], HOMUS [4], and MUSCIMA++ datasets [12] that are available under liberal licenses, and of course the veritable Gamera open-source system [14]. However, there is not enough effort to ensure that data formats are inter-operable, evaluation procedures are shared among authors, and in general that the wheel does not get reinvented for every experiment.

A further critical missing piece for interoperability is the lack of a practical format for OMR-oriented structured representation of music notation. There is ongoing work in the MEI community[2], but it has limited reach. The MusicXML format, which is the *de facto* standard for music notation interchange, and MNX, its successor[3] project led by the W3C Music Notation Community Group[3], are moving towards a broader standardization as well. However, both MEI and MusicXML/MNX are not very suitable for storing intermediate OMR information, as they mix together the graphical elements of music notation and the abstract musical objects that are encoded by them. There have been attempts to create a format tailored for OMR output [5,12,15], but so far none of them has actually become a standard.

A conclusion from this point of discussion is that an annual or biannual workshop centered on OMR that brings together its practitioners and stakeholders (and, to gain critical size, incorporating related "systems for reading music" — score following, cross-modal retrieval, and also music notation typesetting

---

[1] https://github.com/audiveris.

[2] http://music-encoding.org/.

[3] https://www.w3.org/community/music-notation.

software) should be organized to intensify collaboration within the OMR community, and build relationships to its stakeholders. This can be done at relatively low costs. Establishing personal contact and collaboration with digital musicology and digital libraries will also be necessary to sustain funding for OMR-related projects in the future.

4 Outlook

The GREC'17 workshop in Kyoto provided the OMR community with a unique opportunity to meet and discuss together the broad non-technical challenges the field is facing, which have unfortunately been somewhat neglected thus far. There are clear "action items" that the community should take upon itself to resolve:

- Revisit the way OMR talks about itself, specifically with the focus on a taxonomy of OMR systems according to their goals and outputs and accompanying evaluation metrics.
- Intensify collaboration within the OMR community and with related fields, preferably by creating a publication venue where stakeholders can naturally learn about each others' needs and use-cases and establish productive collaborations.
- Continue the trend of open-source software and data — make sure to reflect this principle e.g. when reviewing OMR publications.
- Improve music notation representations or at least provide conversion software between widely adopted representations such as MEI or MusicXML and OMR-specific formats.

The discussion group agreed that if this agenda for OMR is followed, the field will see a qualitative improvement that will ultimately benefit everyone involved: the OMR community itself, as well as the composers, musicians, musicologists, librarians, and other stakeholders who are waiting for reliable OMR systems that address their specific needs.

Acknowledgments. Jorge Calvo-Zaragoza acknowledges the support from the Spanish Ministerio de Economía, Industria y Competitividad through Juan de la Cierva - Formación grant (Ref. FJCI-2016-27873). Jan Hajič jr. acknowledges the support by the Czech Science Foundation grant no. P103/12/G084, Charles University Grant Agency grants 1444217 and 170217, and by SVV project 260 453.

References

1. Bainbridge, D., Bell, T.: A music notation construction engine for optical music recognition. Softw. Pract. Exp. **33**(2), 173–200 (2003)
2. Bellini, P., Bruno, I., Nesi, P.: Assessing optical music recognition tools. Comput. Music J. **31**(1), 68–93 (2007)

3. Byrd, D., Simonsen, J.G.: Towards a standard testbed for optical music recognition: definitions, metrics, and page images. J. New Music Res. **44**(3), 169–195 (2014)
4. Calvo-Zaragoza, J., Oncina, J.: Recognition of pen-based music notation: the HOMUS dataset. In: 22nd International Conference on Pattern Recognition, pp. 3038–3043 (2014)
5. Calvo-Zaragoza, J., Rizo, D.: End-to-end neural optical music recognition of monophonic scores. Appl. Sci. **8**(4), 606–629 (2018)
6. Dalitz, C., Droettboom, M., Pranzas, B., Fujinaga, I.: A comparative study of staff removal algorithms. IEEE Trans. Pattern Anal. Mach. Intell. **30**(5), 753–766 (2008)
7. Droettboom, M., Fujinaga, I.: Symbol-level groundtruthing environment for OMR. In: Proceedings of the 5th International Conference on Music Information Retrieval, pp. 497–500 (2004)
8. Fornés, A., Dutta, A., Gordo, A., Lladós, J.: CVC-MUSCIMA: a ground truth of handwritten music score images for writer identification and staff removal. Int. J. Doc. Anal. Recogn. **15**(3), 243–251 (2012)
9. Fujinaga, I.: Exemplar-based learning in adaptive optical music recognition system. In: International Computer Music Conference, pp. 55–56 (1996)
10. Hajič Jr., J., Pecina, P.: Detecting Noteheads in Handwritten Scores with ConvNets and Bounding Box Regression. Computing Research Repository abs/1708.01806 (2017)
11. Hajič Jr., J., Pecina, P.: Groundtruthing (not only) music notation with music-marker: a practical overview. In: 12th International Workshop on Graphics Recognition, pp. 47–48 (2017)
12. Hajič Jr., J., Pecina, P.: The MUSCIMA++ dataset for handwritten optical music recognition. In: 14th IAPR International Conference on Document Analysis and Recognition, pp. 39–46 (2017)
13. Hajič Jr., J., Novotný, J., Pecina, P., Pokorný, J.: Further steps towards a standard testbed for optical music recognition. In: Proceedings of the 17th International Society for Music Information Retrieval Conference, pp. 157–163. New York University (2016)
14. MacMillan, K., Droettboom, M., Fujinaga, I.: Gamera: optical music recognition in a new shell. In: Proceedings of the 2002 International Computer Music Conference (2002)
15. Miyao, H., Haralick, R.M.: Format of ground truth data used in the evaluation of the results of an optical music recognition system. In: IAPR workshop on document analysis systems, pp. 497–506 (2000)
16. Novotný, J., Pokorný, J.: Introduction to optical music recognition: Overview and practical challenges. In: Necasky M., Moravec P., Pokorný, J. (eds.) Proceedings of the Dateso 2015 Annual International Workshop on DAtabases, TExts, Specifications and Objects, vol. 1343, pp. 65–76. CEUR-WS (2015)
17. Pacha, A., Choi, K.Y., Coüasnon, B., Ricquebourg, Y., Zanibbi, R., Eidenberger, H.: Handwritten music object detection: open issues and baseline results. In: 2018 13th IAPR Workshop on Document Analysis Systems (2018)
18. Padilla, V., Marsden, A., McLean, A., Ng, K.: Improving OMR for digital music libraries with multiple recognisers and multiple sources. In: 1st International Workshop on Digital Libraries for Musicology, pp. 1–8 (2014)
19. Rebelo, A., Fujinaga, I., Paszkiewicz, F., Marcal, A.R., Guedes, C., Cardoso, J.S.: Optical music recognition: state-of-the-art and open issues. Int. J. Multimedia Inf. Retrieval **1**(3), 173–190 (2012)

20. Saleh, Z., Zhang, K., Calvo-Zaragoza, J., Vigliensoni, G., Fujinaga, I.: Pixel.js: Web-based pixel classification correction platform for ground truth creation. In: 12th International Workshop on Graphics Recognition, pp. 39–40 (2017)
21. van der Wel, E., Ullrich, K.: Optical music recognition with convolutional sequence-to-sequence models. In: Proceedings of the 18th International Society for Music Information Retrieval Conference, pp. 731–737 (2017)

Discussion Group Summary: Graphics Syntax in the Deep Learning Age

Bertrand Coüasnon[1], Ashok Popat[2], and Richard Zanibbi[3(✉)]

[1] Univ Rennes, CNRS, IRISA, 35000 Rennes, France
`couasnon@irisa.fr`
[2] Google Research, Mountain View, CA 94043, USA
`popat@google.com`
[3] Rochester Institute of Technology, Rochester, NY, USA
`rxzvcs@rit.edu`

Abstract. This document summarizes the discussion of the interest group on Graphics Syntax in the Deep Learning Age that took place in the 12th IAPR International Workshop on Graphics Recognition (GREC).

Keywords: Graphics syntax · Deep learning · Discussion groups

1 Topics of Discussion

Summary

- Deep learning powerful for object detection & parsing natural language.
- Deep learning data-hungry: labeled graphic datasets often small/absent.
- Graphics recognition distinct from text recognition: harder due to 2D vs. 1D input, importance of distant relationships (e.g., key signature in music).
- Maturity of graphics recognition lags behind text recognition. Should these methods be adapted for 2D graphics, or is a different approach needed?
- Where syntax may help: expressing infrequent patterns in an a priori manner (e.g., in a grammar) rather than inferring them using statistical methods (e.g., deep nets): reduce data dependency and model complexity.

Deep learning has produced very good results for object detection and parsing natural language. The discussion started on the specificities of graphics recognition compared to natural language processing: bi-dimensionality; the importance of long-distance relationships; the fact that labeled datasets are often small or absent in graphics, and are very costly to build. As deep learning methods need huge amounts of labeled data, it seems difficult to directly apply them to graphics recognition. Should those methods be adapted for 2D graphics?

As both graphics and natural language are strongly structured by syntax, it seems interesting to answer yes - but it can be hard to find sufficient training data to capture rare long-distant relationships and infer infrequent patterns. Perhaps

A. Fornés and B. Lamiroy (Eds.): GREC 2017, LNCS 11009, pp. 158–162, 2018.
https://doi.org/10.1007/978-3-030-02284-6_13

it is easier to express these less frequently patterns in an a priori manner (e.g, using a grammar). These discussions led to other discussions presented in Sect. 3 on approaches to parsing using deep learning methods, to extend them to 2D, and in Sect. 4 on combining grammatical techniques with deep learning. Before these discussions we had exchanges on 2D structure representations, reported in Sect. 2. Fig. 1 provides a picture of our discussion group.

Fig. 1. Our discussion group at GREC 2017

2 2D Structure Representations

Summary

- **Comment.** Few representations for graphics structure include cycles. We did not identify non-hierarchical outputs used for graphics recognition.
- Unique ground truth graphs definable when input primitives over-segment recognition targets and are small in number (e.g., PDF symbols, handwritten strokes with at most one symbol).
    - Can use labeled adjacency ('lg') graphs with label *sets* on nodes and edges (per CROHME [1] competitions) for graphs with or without cycles.
    - All differences between 'lg' graphs directly identifiable, measurable through *input primitives* fixed across recognition algorithms. Tools available.[1]
    - Possible future work: develop learning/parsing methods over 'lg' graphs.
- When exactly matching ground truth impractical (e.g., symbol detection in images), can still compute exact differences in output graphs, but target matching must be approximate (e.g., thresholding intersection-over-union vs. identical locations).

---

[1] CROHME LgEval library: https://www.cs.rit.edu/~dprl/Software.html.

- May prevent direct learning from 'lg' graphs in this case... future work?
- Editable representations (e.g., CAD, XML) help design & development, provide synthetic training data.

Representation of 2D graphics structure is important for outputs of recognition, ground truth, evaluation, constructing training data, etc. We observed that few representations for graphics structure include cycles and we did not identify non-hierarchical outputs used for graphics recognition. It was pointed out that it is possible to build unique ground truth graphs when input primitives over-segment recognition targets and are small in number, as with handwritten strokes or PDF symbols. An example label graph was demonstrated for the math expression $2 + 3^x$ (see Fig. 2 on the whiteboard). Tools exist that identify and evaluate *all* differences between ground truth and output representations. Possible future work includes learning/parsing methods operating directly upon label graphs.

However, when recognition targets are, for example, symbols detected in images, exact differences in output graphs is still possible but target must be approximated with, for example, intersection-over-union (IoU), label graphs may not be used for learning. This could be explored as future work.

The possibility of generating synthetic training data by viewing the recognition problem as the inverse or dual of graphics authoring, suggests using an editable authoring representation as the output representation of recognition. In particular, vast amounts of training labeled data could then be generated by rendering and distorting instances of the output representation, e.g., using some CAD or desktop publishing XML schema. Coupled with an end-to-end deep learning recognizer, this approach could recover a particularly useful level of semantics, namely that at which a human author would operate.

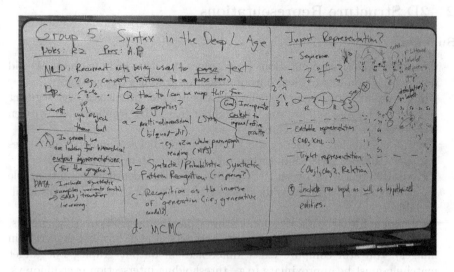

Fig. 2. The whiteboard after our discussion

3   Approaches to Parsing Using Deep Learning Methods

Summary

- **Questions.** Can we extend methods for 1D data to 2D? Or is a distinct approach needed - can syntactic pattern recognition techniques be extended/ combined with deep learning?
- **Opinion.** Benefit in deep methods in part from increased reliance upon raw input data (and continuous features) vs. *inferred* discrete entities used in syntactic pattern recognition (e.g., parsing using *recognized* symbols).
- NLP: using recurrent nets to parse text: sentence → parse tree.
- Sequential methods (e.g., LSTM) lose 2D context. Multi-dimensional LSTMs improve this, still do not interpret directly within 2D input space.
- Opportunities
  - Exploiting correlations in feature maps (e.g., a2ia paragraph reading modules use multi-directional LSTMS).
  - Constrain problems (e.g., in steps, output graph detail).
  - Use loss function forcing network to learn to solve the problem (e.g., identifying target graph).
  - Develop *generative models* - clean synthetic data can be helpful for this.

Several questions were asked about the possibility to extend deep learning-based parsing methods from 1D to 2D, and about the possible combination of syntactic pattern recognition and deep learning techniques. One of the most compelling properties of deep methods is their ability to learn features and to work from raw input data; syntactic pattern recognition methods use discrete recognized symbols, generating difficulties arising from making hard decisions early (e.g., for segmentation) and the rapid explosion in combinations when alternative hypotheses are explored. To extend from 1D to 2D, we discussed first recurrent networks, which which are used to parse text (1D) in Natural Language Processing. Recurrent networks such as LSTM lose 2D context, but have been extended to multi-dimensional (MD)LSTM to try to integrate more bi-dimensional information. They still do not use the full 2D input space directly, and instead register/align 1D views.

Some opportunities were discussed including exploiting correlations in feature maps for paragraph reading with multi-directional LSTMs, the definition of loss functions adapted for 2D parsing, and developing generative models using synthetic data.

4   Combining Grammatical Techniques with Deep Learning

Summary

- Preserving uncertainty about hypotheses (i.e., 'weak decisions,' 'late commitment').

- Interface at the triplet level? (object1, object2, relation).
- Strategy: identify sub-problems which are data driven, and where *lots of data is available*.
  - Training Data/Data Expansion (e.g., GAN, transfer learning).
  - Strategy: use grammars to define rare/distant language elements that are hard to infer from data.

The last discussion was on the combination of grammatical techniques with deep learning. This combination offers the possibility to limit the use of grammars to elements for which labeled data is scarce, or where long distance relationships are needed. When sufficient training data is available to infer (probabilistic) syntax reliably, it makes sense to use deep learning techniques. Even more when data is not available, grammars can provide a way to generate training data and complex contextual information for deep learning. For example, grammars can contextually select sub-regions of the graphic document associated with a contextually reduced vocabulary, to make possible application of techniques like GAN (Generative Adversarial Networks) to automatically generate datasets for future training, or application of data expansion. The combination can also allow a simplification of the grammar definition, in particular offloading segmentation tasks to deep learning modules.

Acknowledgements. We thank the GREC organizers for hosting this event, and all the discussion participants for an engaging and animated discussion.

References

1. Mouchère, H., Viard-Gaudin, C., Zanibbi, R., Garain, U.: ICFHR2016 CROHME: competition on recognition of online handwritten mathematical expressions. In: 2016 15th International Conference on Frontiers in Handwriting Recognition (ICFHR), pp. 607–612, October 2016

Two Decades of GREC Workshop Series. Conclusions of GREC2017

Josep Lladós(✉) ⓘD

Computer Vision Center and Computer Science Department,
Universitat Autònoma de Barcelona, 08193 Catalonia, Bellaterra, Spain
Josep.Llados@cvc.uab.cat
http://www.cvc.uab.cat

Abstract. This paper summarizes the conclusions drawn in the panel discussion of the Graphics Recognition Workshop (GREC2017) held in Kyoto, Japan in November 2017. As usual, GREC was an exciting workshop with lots of interactions between attendees. Graphics Recognition community is evolving. It is no longer a compact community focused on typical problems as vectorization, text-graphics separation, or symbol recognition. Instead, Graphics Recognition is now a confluence of research problems from different areas with the common interest of interpreting symbolic constructions that follow a context-dependent language.

Keywords: Graphics Recognition · GREC workshop · IAPR-TC10

1 Retrospective: Twenty Years of GREC Workshops

1.1 The Concept of Graphics Recognition

In a traditional view, the field of Document Image Analysis and Recognition has been roughly divided in two major subareas, namely text and graphics recognition. From this point of view where the criterion is the type of information that is extracted from document images, Graphics Recognition can be stated as the subfield of Document Analysis aiming to process documents containing diagrammatic notations. Diagrammatic notations are human communication messages basically consisting of terms such as textual labels, lines and arcs, loops, solid regions, dotted lines, hatched patterns, etc. combined in terms of bi-dimensional rules depending on the domain. Originally, the main categories of graphical documents were engineering drawings, architectural floor plans, and maps. Thus, the main purposes were the conversion of raster images after scanning (large) paper documents into CAD and GIS formats.

Thank you to all the attendees to GREC2017 workshop for their valuable contributions during the final panel session.
The author was financially supported by projects CONCORDIA (TIN2015-70924-C2-2-R) and XARXES (2016ACUP-00008), and the CERCA Program/Generalitat de Catalunya.

A. Fornés and B. Lamiroy (Eds.): GREC 2017, LNCS 11009, pp. 163–168, 2018.
https://doi.org/10.1007/978-3-030-02284-6_14

1.2   The Evolution of GREC Workshops: A Keywords Perspective

The first edition of the Graphics Recognition Workshop, endorsed by the Technical Committee 10 of the International Association of Pattern Recognition (IAPR), was held at Penn State University, USA, in 1995. Table 1 compiles the intensity of the different contributions in the proceedings regarding the main topics.

Table 1. Papers by Topic in GREC Workshops.

	1995	1997	1999	2001	2003	2005	2007	2009	2011	2013	2015	2017
Low-level processing	16%	7%	0%	10%	6%	6%	0%	0%	8%	13%	0%	0%
Vectorization, primitive extraction, text-graphics	16%	13%	10%	16%	6%	19%	17%	17%	5%	4%	16%	15%
Technical drawings & maps	21%	30%	29%	19%	18%	0%	9%	3%	8%	21%	8%	9%
Layout analysis & diagrammatic notations, music	16%	13%	6%	13%	3%	8%	3%	10%	11%	0%	24%	39%
Applications, systems & architectures	0%	13%	10%	13%	12%	6%	0%	3%	3%	13%	8%	6%
Symbol & shape recognition	11%	13%	23%	6%	18%	25%	14%	17%	18%	8%	8%	12%
Retrieval, indexing & spotting	5%	0%	6%	10%	15%	11%	14%	14%	5%	13%	4%	0%
Sketching, handwritten graphics	0%	0%	3%	0%	10%	18%	8%	11%	10%	16%	13%	12%	3%
Performance evaluation	16%	10%	13%	3%	6%	6%	17%	10%	13%	13%	16%	9%
Historical documents	0%	0%	0%	0%	0%	11%	14%	14%	8%	0%	0%	3%
Camera-based graphics	0%	0%	0%	0%	0%	0%	0%	0%	5%	4%	4%	3%

A first glance analysis of this table leads us to draw the following musings. First, the traditionally considered graphics recognition problems (vectorization, text-graphics separation and symbol recognition) are still there. They are not with the same strength than in the first editions of the workshop, but there is still some research addressed to improve the state of the art, in general in a given context (e.g. symbol recognition in a particular application). We observe an increase in the works on systems for specific document types with diagrammatic notation, in particular tables, flow charts, music scores, etc. This is probably driven by the needs of the market concerning applications for massive reading of certain types of documents. Surprisingly, the traditional document types like engineering drawings, electronic diagrams, maps, etc. seem to decay. These type of documents are nowadays digitally born, therefore the traditional raster-to-vector conversion to import scanned line drawings to CAD and GIS systems is a mature problem from the scientific point of view. Performance evaluation is always present. The community requires standard and open databases and ground truth, and with the increase of the use of machine learning methods, training data is always needed.

Two particular application areas are recovering protagonism: comics and Optical Music Recognition (OMR). We can not consider them genuinely Graphics Recognition problems, and these topics have their own communities. But the links to Graphics Recognition are evident, so they deserve an increasing centrality. It is surprising that sketch-based systems have a low impact in GREC. It is another example of an area of interest that has a research community, but probably it has stronger ties with the domains of Human-Computer Interfaces, and Computer Graphics than with Document Analysis. It is a challenge for our community in the future, to strengthen the links to this community, and contribute with graphical symbol recognition methods to solve problems of these domains.

1.3   Main Conclusions Drawn in GREC2017

Conclusion 1: In GREC2017 we noticed that. Graphics Recognition is a component in end-to-end interpretation systems (machines as message decoders where graphical languages are an important but not unique component).

The traditional steps (vectorization, text/graphics separation, symbol recognition) are still there but they are losing strength by themselves. However they make sense in a global pipeline. If we analyze them individually, the state of the art is close to consider the problems are solved. The inclusion of traditional topics in a broader context that requires semantic interpretation in a given context (e.g. music scores, diagrams, engineering drawings, maps) is more challenging.

Conclusion 2: Graphics Recognition in more global end-to-end systems. As researchers, there is a need to escape from our comfort zone, where we are designing ad-hoc methods for particular problems. From a semiotic point of view, the field will move from the signifier (recognition of the compounding symbols) to the significant, i.e. the reading and understanding of the sign system in the context where it appears.

There is a need to incorporate more semantics into the process. We are in the artificial intelligence era, where machines understand and act. Graphical objects are understood in terms of a language and a context. There is a need to cope with genericity and heterogeneity, so the systems must learn and adapt themselves to different contexts, not to be designed for ad-hoc for each use case. Graphics Recognition has to be seen as a service that should be offered to several interpretation pipelines. On another hand, systems must be scalable and allow large scale interpretation.

Conclusion 3: Graphics Recognition in the Deep Era. As in textual objets (OCR, HTR, NLP) language models have been integrated in deep learning architectures, the integration of bidimensional language models is a challenge for the next years.

As in the other areas, Deep Neural Networks have irrupted in Graphics Recognition. But is it the silver bullet? Do we really need it for everything? When designing a system, we have to take into account the cost of learning (training data). Graphical documents involve 2D visual languages. In textual input decoding, LSTM+CTC models have been successfully incorporated so they allow to keep memory of the context, i.e. the syntactical structure of the sentence. Graphical constructions usually involve bidimensional languages, which difficult the training process. Paradigms like Graph Neural Networks are promising frameworks to take into account.

Conclusion 4: the need of annotated data. We have to take advantage of the effort made by the community and centralize data and protocols (e.g. the Engineering Drawings Challenge). The role of the TC10/TC11 dataset curators is essencial to define the roadmap for data generation.

A big amount of ground truth data is required, not only for performance evaluation, but also for training. In addition to classical ways of generating data (crowdsourcing) there are new challenging directions to consider: data augmentation, synthetic generation.

2   Current Trends and Challenges

Graphics Recognition is currently present in many problems and applications that involve the interpretation of graphical languages. In addition to the traditional topics that we use to see at GREC workshops, there are interesting problems that are becoming attractive. In this section, we briefly overview these problems and challenges, according to the discussions held during GREC2017.

Graphics-rich document understanding, especially in large-scale scenarios, is a market need. Organizations have digital mail room workflows, where heterogeneous documents, both paper-based and digitally born, have to be processed. The understanding of the contents are required by business intelligence systems. In addition to traditional graphical documents such as engineering drawings, graphical components like logos, stamps, or even tables provide rich information. Components addressed to recognize graphical parts are integrated in ERP and data analytics software.

Flowchart and diagram recognition is a particular type of graphical language that is intensively addressed. Big companies are developing parsing tools for these specific structures. The interpretation of diagrams is useful in different types of applications, as a matter of example, diagrams are efficient communication instruments in scientific papers, in chemical industry, or in patents. In patent interpretation, flowchart interpretation is a useful mechanism to validate or search purposes. A well known challenge for flowchart interpretation in patent documents has been organized since 2009 [3].

The advent of pen or touch-screen based interfaces has increased the interest for **sketch recognition**. Not only for on-line handwriting, which has been a research topic since decades ago, but also for graphical inputs that are the communication language in many emerging applications. The use of sketches in multimodal processing tools has become popular. Sketch-based image retrieval [8] is a growing challenge among the scientific community of computer vision and pattern recognition. Ellis et al. [4] proposed a model that learns to convert simple hand drawings into graphics programs written in a subset of LaTeX.

Doodling in touch screens in smartphones has open a myriad of applications and services. The use of doodles as a simple way to communicate ideas can be used in retrieval, design, education, security, etc. Graphical passwords for user authentificaton is a clear use case that offers flexibility, simplicity and security [6]. Doodling experiences have been proposed online by big companies [1], [2].

These platforms, offered as toy apps, allow to collect many samples from different uses and construct a big ground truth for the community.

Logo Recognition as a particular case of symbol recognition has been one of the central topics of Graphics Recognition. We can observe that beyond the typical application of logo recognition for document classification, there are new applications related to new business services. Brand analysis through social networks is an important issue in marketing departments of companies. An efficient mechanism to track the popularity of the products of a brans is to search for the corresponding logos in the different medias that users publish in social networks. In addition, companies are concerned in forgeries of their brand icons. Scientifically, this is an interesting challenge involving logo detection and classification on the wild. The need of logo databases for training is a crucial need, not only to have instances of real logos but to teach machines to find logos in real scenes. An interesting logo database have been synthetically generated using Generative Adversarial Networks (GAN) [7].

Finally, the literature shows other interesting applications of Graphics Recognition. In [5], Graphics Recognition is used in a multimodal Question Answering system in an educational context. Sixth grade textbooks are analyzed, and the illustrations and diagrams are analyzed together with the textual information. A curious graphics recognition application is graffiti recognition for author identification. It is a forensics problem that has been developed as a tool for Police departments.

3   Final Conclusion and Envisioning the Future

Graphical languages are part of the human communication. Together with textual information, graphical symbols construct messages made by humans to be understood by humans, in the context where they appear. Documents as containers of compound signs, are no longer static paper-based sources, but have evolved to multi-media platforms. Document Analysis has evolved to Reading Systems, in the widest sense. Nowadays, robust reading, sketching interfaces, on-line signature verification, etc. are well-known problems addressed by the document analysis community but they are far from being constrained to process scanned paper documents. The community has open the scope shifting from the object (document images) to the function (interpreting symbols made by humans). Graphics Recognition is aligned with this move. Therefore, the community of Graphics Recognition nowadays is no longer a small but compact group of researchers working on vectorization, text-graphics separation, symbol recognition, etc. but is more a confluence of people coming from different areas (document analysis, computer vision, human-computer interaction, optical music recognition, etc.) that share the interest of interpreting visual (usually bidimensional) languages in their respective fields. Thus, we are now more concerned in methodologies and their application to interpret graphical entities in end-to-end systems.

In conclusion, we see the future of Graphics Recognition as part of global reading systems, i.e. end-to-end systems for interpreting human-made visual messages. These messages are constructed following a language that is valid in a particular context. The support for these messages can range from the traditional document images to other types of media, including digitally born documents. The Graphics Recognition Workshop held every two years as a satellite event of the International Conference on Document Analysis and Recognition (ICDAR) will attract the interest of researchers from different communities having as common interest the development of techniques for parsing graphical sentences. Methods for graphics recognition will be general enough to adapt themselves to different scenarios and learn incrementally. The need for annotated data will increase in the future, as in other domains of Pattern Recognition. Thus, mechanisms for sharing, compiling, annotating or synthetically generate data will be a relevant focus of attention.

References

1. Autodraw. https://www.autodraw.com/
2. Google quick draw. https://quickdraw.withgoogle.com/
3. CLEF-IP: Retrieval in the intellectual property domain (2009). http://www.ifs. tuwien.ac.at/~clef-ip/
4. Ellis, K., Ritchie, D., Solar-Lezama, A., Tenenbaum, J.: Learning to infer graphics programs from hand-drawn images. CoRR abs/1707.09627 (2017). http://arxiv.org/ abs/1707.09627
5. Kembhavi, A., Seo, M., Schwenk, D., Choi, J., Farhadi, A., Hajishirzi, H.: Are you smarter than a sixth grader? textbook question answering for multimodal machine comprehension. In: 2017 IEEE Conference on Computer Vision and Pattern Recognition (CVPR), pp. 5376–5384, July 2017. https://doi.org/10.1109/CVPR.2017.571
6. Martínez-Díaz, M., Fiérrez, J., Galbally Herrero, J.: Graphical password-based user authentication with free-form doodles. IEEE Trans. Hum.-Mach. Syst. **46**(4), 607–614 (2016). https://doi.org/10.1109/THMS.2015.2504101
7. Sage, A., Agustsson, E., Timofte, R., Van Gool, L.: Logo synthesis and manipulation with clustered generative adversarial networks. CoRR abs/1712.04407 (2017). http://arxiv.org/abs/1712.04407
8. Sangkloy, P., Burnell, N., Ham, C., Hays, J.: The sketchy database: learning to retrieve badly drawn bunnies. ACM Trans. Graph. **35**(4), 119 (2016)

Author Index

Author Index

Printed in the United States
By Bookmasters